Who Knows Who?

Also by the Author

The Hampshire Hogs History (1987) Potwell Press
Think Cricket (2001) Empire Publications
Plan Cricket (2003) Potwell Press
Think Cricket 2nd Edition (2011) G2 Entertainment

WHO KNOWS WHO?
First published 2011
Jellyfish Publishing Services,
Suite B, 1st Floor, Hollythorns House,
The Hollythorns,
New Road, Swanmore SO32 2NW
Tel: 01489 897373

© Christopher Bazalgette 2011

ISBN: 978-1-907803-80-2

Typesetting and Production by Jellyfish Print Solutions Ltd.
www.jellyfishsolutions.co.uk

British Library Cataloguing in Publication Data
a catalogue record for this book is available at the British Library

Who Knows Who?

by
Christopher Bazalgette

<small>EDITED BY</small>
Ivo Tennant
(Cricket Correspondent for the *Times*)

<small>FOREWORD BY</small>
David Gower OBE

ACKNOWLEDGEMENTS

There are many who deserve my thanks in writing this book, for it is not just the preparation, praise is due to those who trained and encouraged me along the road.

First I must thank the professionals who supported my early writings – Christopher Martin-Jenkins, Reg Hayter, Irving Rosenwater, Mandy Ripley and Ben Brocklehurst.

This book's strength is due largely to the inclusion of those who have profiles written about them, to them and their profilers I am very grateful:

Pat Jessop, Robin Brodhurst, Henriette Turner, Patrick Eagar, Peter Haslop, Julian Shackleton, Andrew Johnston, Christopher Cowdrey, Ben Neely, Ann White, Bill Hughes, Keith Moss, Rob Kitson, Rowly Potter, Hamesh Solomons, Richard Merricks, Patrick Maclure, Andrew Renshaw, Judy Vigors, Ross Edwards, Bill Tyrwhitt-Drake, George Gordon-Smith, Nigel French, John Barclay, Nick Syrett, Simon Tuke, Andrew Longmore, Paul Lawrence and Denis Jenkinson.

I also would like to thank Andrea Gordon, Juliet Parker and Jennifer Beddis for finding and gaining permission to use the interview with Sacha Ben Cohen in his guise as Borat in the Ali G show.

My very special thanks go to Ivo Tennant for his advice and guidance apart from his professional editing of the book.

Similarly, I thank Ian Broughton volunteering to do the onerous task of proof reading, and to Mark Williams and BT Home Advisor for conquering my computer.

Everybody has excelled in supporting this publication, no less than David Gower in agreeing to write the Foreword despite having the side issues of commentating on the England tour of Australia and the World Cup ODI competition at the same time.

To Jocelyn Galsworthy and Tim Munton for thoughts on promotion and Michael Massey for his faith in me and finally my wife, June for tirelessly supporting my cricket, our partnership in love, indexing this book and keeping me focussed.

CONTENTS

HRH The Queen Mother with her jockey Bill Smith after he had gained his 30th winner, riding the Queen Mother's horse Special Cargo.

INTRODUCTION

Who Knows Who? is an autobiography with a difference, for although it traces my life, it is concerned more with the famous people I have known. Each one has a profile written about him or her, by either myself, a journalist or one of their friends or relations. Where the subject of the profile is very famous, the writer has been asked to show a more private side.

Many of those who have been profiled have had their own setbacks and challenges and it is only through their dedication and determination that they have eventually won through. I am a firm believer that you should always treat people as they treat you, therefore I make no apology for the fact that those I have chosen to profile are good people who are friends of mine. Hence this is not a book that casts aspersions, but one that recognises their achievements and successes.

Most of my life has been centred within cricket and hence most of the connections have come from a cricketing base. But there are excursions into rugby, water-skiing, motor and horse racing, plus Antarctic exploration, the Army and journalism. The decision as to whom to choose to profile has been mine alone. I have been privileged to know many famous people and I have opted in the main for those who are still alive, with the exception of some superstars.

FOREWORD

In an era when most sporting books come from the "pen" of a game's more illustrious participants here is a fascinating and honourable exception. Many of the names you will come across within these covers are indeed famous but the author himself, though undoubtedly known by many in cricket's broader circles, is yet to make his Test debut! Christopher, though, has taken a staggering number of wickets, knows the county of Hampshire and its club and league cricket better than anyone, and indeed has come across a great variety of people within the game, so he is particularly well qualified to weave all this information into this unique form of autobiography. I did play with and against some of his subjects and contributors and to this day Chris Cowdrey remains one of my oldest friends. Of course I share a commentary box – and a love of good wines – with Ian Botham, while Robin Smith was a colleague at county and Test level and John Barclay a wily opposition captain.

I do not claim to have the most extensive cricket library or a definitive collection of memorabilia but I have always enjoyed insightful writing on the game and who better to cite in that category than the sage of Longparish, John Woodcock, who is another of Christopher's subjects. Some of the older names who are no longer with us, such as Ben Brocklehurst, I knew in a tangential way, and it is interesting to learn more about them and their considerable contributions to cricket and other areas of life.

Chris Cowdrey's account of his own father, Colin, is a wonderful study, both perceptive and amusing. I have known Chris since we played rugby against each other at school – I was at King's Canterbury and he was at Tonbridge but the schools had had one of those tiffs that schools do and sadly had long since ceased meeting on the cricket field– but I could not begin to appreciate the expectations that were heaped on him at a young age on account of being the son of the England captain. Yet he survived, played Test cricket himself and has never moaned about the comparisons – not even when a Kent supporter came up to him in the bar after making a Benson & Hedges Cup century on his debut in that competition and told him: 'Your father made one in his first match too, didn't he?'

I might well have played for Kent at the start of my career, for I was born in Tunbridge Wells, or even later on after I left Leicestershire, when it was the one other county I considered joining aside from Hampshire. It could have been a sort of homecoming but home is now very much Hampshire after twenty plus years and that is where I transferred my loyalty then and where it still lies now.

In fact I first met Christopher before my move to his county, when he signed me up for his single wicket competition in 1979 and we have continued to come across each other down the years at matches and at dinners. I have never had to face his bowling; had I had to do so it is odds on he would have claimed me as one of his many victims. No-one takes as many wickets as he for the Hampshire Hogs without a certain canniness or a degree of longevity! Not many bowlers tossed the ball up above the eye line in my time; far too many seemed to be mostly aiming at my head! He tells me that but for a field change in one particular fixture, he might have held on to what he says was a stinging drive. That was some time ago now, I might add, for it is many a year since I have played cricket at any level. There are many excuses; all those commentary boxes, some finely crafted words now and again for the *Sunday Times*, following my daughters in their own sporting endeavours – hockey, netball but no cricket! And – the crunch – I just have no will left to play the game that has admittedly given me huge satisfaction and joy over the years. I just like looking at it now from a different angle.

There are still some very nice but probably over optimistic folk who will approach me and suggest that I should still be out there with a bat in hand and that, of course, is nice to hear. But most ex-professionals feel as I do – we have played first-class sport for 20 years and the time has come to do something else. Through my job with SkySports I keep in good contact with developments in the game and with those whom I played against and that is pretty much all I ask.

I expect that other people will also tell me that I can empathise with the subjects herein because many, if not all of them, had a perspective on life that did not merely encompass a bat and a ball. Look at the range of Ian Botham's enthusiasms and beware that there is no such thing as a half hearted approach to anything for Ian. Think of Field Marshall Lord Bramall's contributions beyond the boundary. A cricketer can become too focused on the professional side of his life and thus worn down by relentless travel, nets and matches. Those I have fundamentally admired have had a sense of perspective.

If I had my time again, would I be a cricketer? Absolutely. I once supposedly had a choice between cricket and the law. In truth the law and I did not see eye to eye and what turned out to be my one year at university was productive only on the hockey field. I have long since stopped wondering whether I might have made a decent or even half decent barrister or solicitor. Following the sun holds its own special appeal! The game seemed more fun than working when I was deciding what to do next in my student days. Mind you, I'm glad I played when I did. Late night Twenty20 contests might have finished me off completely! Best to observe nowadays from the boundary's edge and to settle back – preferably with a glass of Lynch Bages, which I know Christopher would enjoy as much as I do – and peruse this highly enjoyable book.

David Gower

CHAPTER 1

Early Days

Who was the greatest cricket all rounder?

This is the story of a man without influence or prejudice who followed an ideal, the hurdles along the way and the joy that was gained through the medium of the noble game of cricket.

It is more about whom he met and their specific characters than the man himself. But the plan is to show that even though your aims are not necessarily achieved, you can still enjoy the journey and sometimes the unknown result is greater than is anticipated. It will also show from the profiles of the people he met that those who had early ideals and pursued them with determination, despite various drawbacks, won through in the end.

The journey started on the outbreak of the 2nd World War, when he was born overlooking the Edgbaston Cricket Ground, in Birmingham. His mother had been taught by Archie (A.C.) MacLaren and she became his greatest influence, mainly because father was fighting in the Army and away from parental duties.

The name Bazalgette was first recorded as early as 723 AD. One forebear commanded the French Army who repelled the Moors who had swept through Spain, hence their family crest which is a Lion Rampant with its paw on a crescent (the sign of the Moors). The Family's chateau was at

Ispagnac, a little further south of a commune called La Bazalgette.

Christopher's grandfather was Rector of Monk Soham, his great grandfather the famous engineer Sir Joseph Bazalgette, who eradicated typhoid and cholera from the Thames and was responsible for the London sewage system and whose bust stands on the Victoria Embankment. His great, great grandfather was a Naval commander in the Napoleonic era. During the war his cousin, Ian Willoughby, gained a posthumous VC flying as a Pathfinder. Being the youngest of his part of the family, his three half brothers have all died, but he is extremely proud of their children, who have been highly successful in their careers.

Christopher's early schooling was minimal before 1945 and then only a first school with no sport. So the organised cricket did not come prior to the age of nine other than playing in the back garden. But the seed had been sown. The next move at 11 brought him into touch with the real game and even though the formative years had been skimped from an academic or scholastic front, his cricket had developed. The family had moved to Southampton: Hampshire County Cricket Club was to become the launching pad.

Oakmount Preparatory School was fortunate to have 'Lofty' Herman as their coach; he was a very special link with the future, shaping the young man into an opening bowler who could bat as well. The first X1 cricketers were encouraged to attend Easter coaching sessions at the County Ground. Our young man had Johnny Arnold, the double international for cricket and football as his first county coach, ably supported by the 'coach,' Arthur Holt. This was to become probably the happiest time of the young man's life, for he met and became friends with all the Hampshire county squad. His best friend was son of the second XI's captain, Basil Bowyer, and the two travelled to 'home' matches with the players and scored for the second XI. He played in a first X1 training match at the age of 13 and fielded at cover point, a position he loved for all of his youth. He was happy to field in some cases for both sides if the opportunity arose.

He was to know many of the cricketers well. One of the boys also attending nets was Christopher Van der Noot, who rose to become Defence Attache in Chile, and, 60 years later, shares the running of golf days for the Hampshire Hogs Cricket Club with our man.

His first famous meeting came early in the 1949 season when Colin Ingleby-Mackenzie had his trial at Northlands Road. On hand was the Hampshire chairman, Harry Altham, and they played catch together.

Another friend was Hampshire's captain and secretary, Desmond Eagar, who taught the youngster the art of spin bowling and close catching. Heady days continued with the beginnings of friendships with Malcolm Heath, Alan Rayment, Jimmy Gray, Vic Cannings, Derek Shackleton and Neville Rogers. Each would become a lifelong friend.

A quiet period followed with the move, first, to Allhallows School, in Devon, and then another move to Hardye's School in Dorchester, under the wing of Walter Lancashire. This brought an opportunity to meet one of the greatest English cricketers of all time – G.L.Jessop (the Croucher) who resided locally. Who, even though he lived in a block of houses, had enough space in his garden to have a net, so he could coach local youngsters at no cost.

School cricket with colts, second and first XI's was followed by club cricket and the Army, he joined the Household Cavalry, did his basic training at Windsor, followed by mounted ceremonial duties in London.

On becoming a fully-fledged trooper, Christopher mounted guard at Whitehall and carried out escort duty to Her Majesty. He captained the Household Cavalry Regiment cricket team, then, just prior to attendance at the Regular Commission's Board, he had a knee injury.

He was to have virtually two years in hospital and five operations on his left knee.

It took three years of determined effort to play, first, rugby and four years before cricket could be considered. But all his previous experience now bore fruit, because his first job, following a disabled discharge with a 50% disability pension, was to become cricket coach at Malsis Preparatory school, whose headmaster was the former England rugby captain Bernard Gadney, based near Keithley, in Yorkshire.

Under his wing he had the son of Ronnie Burnett, then currently Yorkshire's captain. But another minor operation to his left knee put a stop to this activity. Also just before leaving the Army his father had died, following a long illness.

Two years opening Securicor, in Birmingham, was followed by a change of direction and also of career into publishing, this under the wing of another cricketer – Ben Brocklehurst, the former captain of Somerset. This was a major step back to cricket, although at the time nobody was aware of the fact or of the direction this would have on his life. Another profound setback was that his mother died suddenly. She was a person who had guided his life and his cricketing development with great support and encouragement.

In his years prior to his hospitalisation he had been a bowler, but as the afflicted knee was on his leading leg, bowling was out of the question. So he became an opening batsman, not with much success, although there were occasional glimpses of form. One such occasion was opening with Ron Best of Honor Oak for the Space Sellers against the Space Buyers, when they put on 100 for the first wicket against no less a bowler than Jim Laker. Jim was to gain his scalp through a catch at long on, but this association was the start of a long friendship. Captain of the Space Sellers was the Kent wicket-keeper, Arthur Phebey.

Luckily there were many friends who stood by him when his need was greatest; that, combined with challenge of work and family, kept the young man together.

Sport was very important, which meant his dealings with the fairer sex had been neglected. There had been a few sorties, but the girls always played second fiddle. So when he decided to combine a three week business trip with holiday to Europe it seemed quite the norm, and there was no question of him being accompanied. As it turned out after two weeks he was running out of funds, so he returned to Dieppe in case the trip needed to be curtailed. By chance he met an English family returning from holiday in the South of France and noticed their daughter had a very good sense of humour. He saw them onto their ferry, gained more funds from his company on the Monday and was off for another week around Europe.

His business trip had been to sell advertisements to known clients in Germany and France, for which he had done a crash course in both languages prior to the trip.

On returning home he made contact with the daughter and within two weeks the two became engaged. Eight months later they duly tied the knot.

Marriage brought the pair to Hampshire and our fellow joined the local club and The Hampshire Hogs, for which he was proposed by one of his business clients, Arthur Buckham, and seconded by his boss, Ben Brocklehurst. Apart from being Hogs they were both Bradfield Waifs.

He was still an opening bat, but with his legs becoming much stronger, within four years he had started bowling again, but with a changed action.

His slow away swing proved to be very accurate. Brocklehurst invited him to represent him in some matches and his quality improved.

Then the publishing company changed policy and most titles were sold, including the one on which he worked. Although he was part of the deal, this was not a success and after a short time he was to rejoin Brocklehurst, his director, who also had left the company but took with him an old established publication called *The Cricketer*. The year was 1972. Ben, with the research manager, Harry Constantine, had started to develop the old title. Together these three created sponsorships and built circulation and advertising, their team including E.W. 'Jim' Swanton and first David Frith and then Christopher Martin-Jenkins. To our man this was a marriage made in heaven, for daily he would meet those of like mind. Work and play was as one and the journal grew in every sphere to be market leader. Now one regularly met 'greats' who either worked for the manufacturers or who endorsed specific equipment.

This story is not really about the young man, but more about how life can evolve in different ways, often negating youth's desired plan. With determination and willingness to develop one's options there can still be pleasure, achievement and new challenges that are not necessarily evident when the journey starts.

Before we continue, two major events occurred which have not been mentioned as yet. First, he was married in 1965 on a glorious sunny day during a Test Match at Lord's. The service was due to start at 3 pm, so it was not surprising that he was ensconced in the hotel's television room prior to the lunch interval – surprisingly, though, nobody thought to find him there. The stag party, in true Brigade of Guards style, took place in London the night before the wedding.

This was not for the wimps of today. Best man and bridegroom, arriving at 4am, had risen by 8am and ready for an early swim.

The wedding went superbly and the couple drove off to Dover for their honeymoon on the continent. Half way across the channel, June, his wife, was summoned to the purser's office. This was their first parting, for one of the crew had nearly cut off his thumb and required her medical training. The ship returned to Dover, or that is how the story went, so hours later they were reunited. The only other tribulation to occur was the losing of second and third gears just prior to their drive home from Caorle (northern Italy), requiring the need to put their car on the train.

They set up home in Hampshire in the village of Headley. Three years passed and then came the next major event – their daughter was born, a blue eyed, fair- haired beauty, Fiona. She viewed her first cricket match just ten days later.

Her Christening was a very special occasion, performed by former Irish Rugby international, Bishop Pike, at The Guards' Chapel in London in 1968 and afterwards at the home of Hugh Muirhead, the then director of The British Colour Council, in Farnham. Our man was a consultant to the Council, responsible for publishing. Every year they had a cocktail party. At one of these occasions he was presented to Princess Margaret, the Colour Council's patron.

Back to 1972, he had worked with both Brocklehurst and Constantine at Mercury House, which meant that this new development was straightforward in working terms.

As *The Cricketer* was a very small title, our man became self-employed so that he could participate in other activities whilst it was being built up. In 1976 he applied to join MCC as an out player, but after five matches was told he was too old to fulfill his application as a player, but he was elected as a member that year. He was, though, invited by Arthur Holt to join the Forty Club – more about this later.

Gilbert Laird Jessop

By Pat Jessop *(his daughter-in-law)*

It was on August 13, 1902, in the Fifth Test against Australia at the Oval that Gilbert Jessop played what has been described as the greatest innings in the history of cricket. On a difficult pitch and against monumental odds of 50-1 he scored 104 runs out of 139, his hundred coming up in 75 minutes. This was a speed unequalled in Ashes Tests. Such a score was all the more remarkable since to hit a six in this era the ball had to be struck right out of the ground. His innings included an all run five, 17 fours, two threes and 17 singles. Five shots cleared the ropes, four landing on top of the pavilion or Ladies Stand.

We shall never know how many of Jessop's huge number of fours should have been sixes, but there is every reason to believe that no one hit the ball more frequently over the boundary line. Despite the stricter rule, in his long career for Cambridge University, Gloucestershire and England, his 150 longest innings were scored at an average rate of 82 runs per hour, whereas Hobbs, Hammond and Bradman did not exceed 50. No batsman excited spectators to such a degree.

Almost as notable as the Oval innings was his 93 off 63 balls in 70 minutes at Lord's against South Africa in 1907. Here he faced a quartet of bowlers including J.J.Kotze, who was as fast as Harold Larwood, and Bert Vogler, off whom he hit a ball on to the roof of the pavilion.

Gilbert Laird Jessop was the son of a Cheltenham doctor. He attended Cheltenham Grammar School and afterwards Christ's College, Cambridge. In his first match for Gloucestershire he scored four runs off his first ball, 'Well,' said the Doctor (W.G.Grace) 'we've found something this time.' In 1895 he scored 51 out of 53 against Yorkshire in 18 minutes. Wisden chose him as one of the Five Cricketers of the Year in 1898 and wrote, 'We have never produced a batsman of quite the same stamp …never one who in 20 minutes or half an hour entirely changed the fortunes of the game.' All this at a time when his career had barely started.

In 1899 he was selected to play for England chiefly for his ability as a fast bowler. In 1900 he took over the captaincy of Gloucestershire. In his first year of office he scored 2000 runs and took 100 wickets. In 1907 Jessop and George Dennett bowled out Northamptonshire for 12 runs, the equal lowest total in first-class cricket. In his career he took 851 wickets at under 23 apiece.

Some of his highest scores included 233 in 150 minutes for the Rest of England v Yorkshire in 1901, 286 in 175 minutes v Sussex in 1903, 206 in 150 minutes v Nottinghamshire in 1904, 234 in 155 minutes v Somerset in 1905, 240 in 200 minutes v Sussex in 1907. In 1900 he scored 157 (including 29 fours) in 60 minutes against West Indies at Bristol. At Bath v Somerset in 1908 he scored a century in 63 minutes in the first innings and another in 65 minutes in the second.

His most astonishing feat of sustained scoring was at Hastings in 1907 v the Professionals of the South, when he reached 50 in 24 minutes, 100 in 42 minutes, 150 in 63 minutes and 191 in 90 minutes.

There were 11 more hits over the ropes, which, had these been scored under the regulations that were to come into being three years later, would have given him 213 in 90 minutes entertainment.

So it goes on and on, this astounding fast scoring with a frequency which almost becomes monotonous right through to his last first-class century, 116 out of 138 in 60 minutes in 1913, when he reached his hundred in 55 minutes. There was then no annual award for the fastest century. If there had been he would have had a hundred to offer for consideration, scored at between 40 and 60 minutes in no fewer than ten seasons. In four other years his best was between 63 and 67 minutes.

His only slow offering was in 1905 when he made a century against Somerset, taking 80 minutes - but he went on to reach 200 in 130 minutes. As an off side fielder, it could be argued that Jessop has never been matched. He had a tremendous return and could stand deeper than anyone else at extra cover and still stop a run being taken. He took 451 catches and brought off many run outs.

Every ground where he played recorded feats of his phenomenal hitting and fast scoring. The longest hit from the Sydney Cricket Ground was made by him and he is the only batsman to have hit a ball into the Torrens river from the Adelaide Oval. And he was not only an all round cricketer, for he was selected to play hockey and billiards against Oxford. He played soccer for the Casuals and rugby for Gloucester, could run 100 yards in 10.2 seconds, and was a scratch golfer.

In 1916, whilst serving in the Lincolnshire Regiment and suffering from severe lumbago, he was sent to a clinic in Bath. The Radiant Heat Treatment involved total immersion for 30 minutes at a temperature of 210-319 degrees. The patient was placed in a coffin-like structure that steamed up.

If he became uncomfortable, he could raise the lid to get out. By some accident, the catch fell while the attendant had gone away and Jessop was unable to summon assistance. When he was eventually rescued, his heart had been seriously damaged by this terrible ordeal. In a matter of minutes the sporting life of one of the greatest athletes had come to an abrupt end.

For the next 39 years Jessop was to lead a life of very limited activity. He died at his son's vicarage in Dorchester in 1955 and is buried beside the Church of Fordington St George. His grave was restored in 1999. The same year the new Jessop Stand was opened at the County ground in Bristol. Jessop's birthplace was restored in 1974 and renamed Jessop House. There is a blue plaque on his former home at Sunningdale Gardens, Mill Hill. He is the only cricketer who, through the adjective 'Jessopian' has given his name to the language of cricket.

Jessop's innings of 1902 has severally been nominated as one of the top 100 greatest British sports performances of the twentieth century. His name is still living, the legend is still strong. To quote his biographer, Gerald Broadribb, 'We have waited a long time for a second Jessop and I am sure that there will never be one.' The bat and gloves with which Jessop faced the might of the Australian attack in 1902 are now displayed in the museum at Lord's.

Note:

To have gone to school and lived in close proximity and not met him would have been very sad. However, I did meet him and he gave me his autograph. He was of average build and had piercing blue eyes. His handshake was strong and he was interested in speaking to me as well as my parents. When I asked if he could give me any advice, he said: ' Practise and keep practising, it is a wonderful game, keep true to yourself and cricket will be true to you.' I have tried to follow his dictum.

Harry Altham

By Robin Bordhurst *(his Grandson)*

Harry Altham was described by Jim Swanton as "the complete cricketer" and he wrote a chapter about Harry in his first volume of his autobiography, Sort of a Cricket Person. Harry was born in Frimley, Surrey, in 1888, the youngest son of General Sir Edward Altham, a distinguished soldier recalled in 1915 to sort out the administrative chaos at Gallipoli. Harry went to Repton, where he played in the first XI for four years, captaining the outstanding 1908 side. Four members played county cricket that summer, two others were asked to do so but declined, playing in 1909, and a further three were first-class cricketers later. It must rank as amongst the strongest school sides ever.

He went up to Trinity College, Oxford, to read classics, playing for the college side for four years and winning a cricket blue in both 1911 and 1912. In 1913 he started to teach at Winchester and spent the whole of his career there. However, after one year, war intervened and he served for four years in the King's Royal Rifle Corps on the Western Front, being awarded a DSO and an MC. He would never talk about these, claiming that they "came up with the rations." Certainly, the DSO. was awarded when he was a corps staff officer, but the MC was earned early on while on regimental duty. During this war he married Alison Livingstone-Learmonth, and remained blissfully married for the rest of his life. Alison supported him in every aspect of his being.

On the cricket field he played for Hampshire during the summer holidays from 1919 to 1923, making a highest score of 141 against Kent at Canterbury. However, it was a leader of

Harlequins tours throughout the 1920s and 1930s and as a coach that he was to make his first mark on the game. He was an outstanding captain and should probably have captained Oxford in 1912. The Harlequins tours were famous for their high quality cricket and yet enormous fun. As a coach he bowled slowly – or very slowly – but was an inspiring teacher of the game, and was still bowling in the same net in 1963. He served on the MCC committee in the 1930s and in 1949 was asked to chair their cricket enquiry. Out of this came the MCC Cricket Coaching Book, which he wrote with Gubby Allen, the MCC Youth Cricket Association and ESCA, both of which he was president.

He became a housemaster at Winchester in 1925 and should normally have retired in 1940, but due to another world war he remained as housemaster until 1946. In this he was in his element, providing firm, but loving guidance to about 50 boys, all of whom he simply saw as an extension of his family. He educated them in his own beliefs, which were based on a simple, but firm Christian faith, and a natural view that all were to be trusted until they proved otherwise. Each boy had his niche. This love was reciprocated and hardly a day of his retirement went by without a telephone call or a letter from an old boy, or even better, a visit.

In the 1920s he had started writing a history of cricket, which was published initially in *The Cricketer*. Family lore maintains that it was written so as to pay for a nurse for his youngest daughter. It was eventually published as A History Of Cricket – note the lack of a definitive article – in 1926. John Arlott said of it: "It is remarkable for its scope, perception, and mature style." Subsequent volumes were co-authored by Jim Swanton, and it remains among the best histories of the game, if now a trifle outdated. He also wrote many articles for Wisden and other magazines, for The Observer, The World Of Cricket, and many for the Hampshire Handbook.

His principal work for cricket came after he retired from teaching, with his work for MCC and youth cricket in general. He became MCC treasurer in 1950, and few understand the significance of this post. It was (then) effectively deputy president, and he provided the continuity on the committee along with the secretary. With Ronnie Aird and Billy Griffith, he had no secrets and all worked together seamlessly. MCC then was "a private club with a public mission" and effectively ran world cricket. The ICC met only once every year, usually just before or just after the Lord's Test. Harry became president of MCC in 1959-60, and used his presidency to take up the issue of throwing, after a number of incidents during the 1958-59 tour of Australia. He and Gubby Allen persuaded Sir Donald Bradman to come to England for the ICC conference and to thrash out a way of stopping throwing. That they more or less succeeded is evident, and is a tribute to the hard work done by Harry by letter before the meeting. Certainly, the correspondence (in my keeping) is fascinating. He was a very reluctant chairman of selectors in 1954, claiming for the rest of his life that he was the only man to have chosen an England side that had lost to Pakistan. However, he would then fail to add the rider that he did pick the side that retained the Ashes in 1954-55, the first time this had been done since 1932-33, the Bodyline tour of infamous memory. His two critical choices were M.C. Cowdrey and F.H. Tyson, both a triumph of class over form.

A further string to his bow was that he was amongst the finest after-dinner speakers of his generation, rivaled only by Lord Birkett. Hardly a month went by through the winter when he was not speaking at a cricket dinner, and each one was prepared on an individual basis, whether he was chairing the Old Reptonian Cricket Club, speaking at the centenary dinner of Yorkshire Cricket Club, or at the annual dinner of Little Snodsbury. Each was researched, the individuals singled out and the whole club put into the perspective of the global game. Each year he attended the advanced coaching course at Lilleshall and always spoke before dinner on the history of the game – without a note. I have one on CD, from January 1965, and to hear him talk about WG is enthralling and still attention-grabbing. Possibly my favourite was his speech at the Hampshire dinner after they won their first championship in 1961, when the guests added up to a mellow mixture of the greats of a bygone era and the heroes of 1961.

Above all of these many facets, Harry was a devoted family man and friend to so many. He was typical of his generation in that he believed in keeping his relationships alive by writing letters, even if his handwriting was like the proverbial drunken fly crawling over the paper. He wrote to everybody, treating them all equally. To his family he was the head and shoulders of our lives. Living still in a college house – he never owned his own – Kingsmead was a perfect reflection of him. Down in the cellar was "The Den," which was his study, with a few half windows. Here was where he did his writing and his research, and where he kept his cricket library. Upstairs was the drawing room, redolent of his tobacco. He kept it in a large Persian pot with a spill by the fire from which to light his pipe. This was a lengthy process involving much tamping down, sucking in of air and smoke, and once it was drawing well was put down. At least that was how it seemed to a young grandson. In the corner was a beautifully lit cabinet with his pride and joy, a Chinese Tang horse, and other splendid Chinoiserie, on which he would expound if you wanted him to (but only if you wanted). There was an 1881 statue of Disraeli, carved from the last remaining piece of H.M.S. Bellerophon, to which Napoleon had surrendered in 1815, and there were coloured slides of stained glass. Much of this shows the many varied aspects of his interests. He was the busiest man I knew as a young child, but he always had time for everybody. He was the best guide to Winchester Cathedral and always introduced tourists to the memorial to Piers Gaveston's father as him being the father of the founder of English cricket. He was chairman of the Friends of Winchester Cathedral for many years and annually took my father's class round the cathedral as well as Dennis Silk's class from Marlborough. Such outings had a memorable effect on those privileged to be on them.

He died in Sheffield in March 1965, having just spoken to the Sheffield Cricket Lovers Society at the request of John Hampshire. He had been warned by his doctor to "take things easier" earlier in the year, but had confided to Bob Barber, a typical protégé, that he had no intention of doing so. The memorial service was held in the cathedral, and I can still remember as a 13 year-old how amazed I was by the size of the congregation. Now that I know more about him I am not at all surprised, but to me he remains still the same simple "Grandpa" who taught me how to play cricket and was a loving presence throughout my young days. When I look at the Altham Memorial Gates at Winchester College and the view across the first XI pitch and towards the water meadows and St. Catherine's Hill, or at the memorial stone at Lord's in the museum, I remain humbled by how much he achieved, and by how little I have done.

Bernard Gadney

By Christopher Bazalgette

The son of an antiquarian who sold books in Oxford, Bernard was educated at The Dragon School and then went to Stowe. He was a natural sportsman, was captain of the first XV and also represented the school at cricket (later playing minor counties cricket for Oxfordshire). While at Stowe he shared a room with David Niven.

Bernard won a scholarship to Oxford University but was unable to attend owing to the failure of the family business. Instead, he worked at a Tannery in Bermondsey, while playing rugby for Richmond. It did not take him long to realise that teaching would suit him better, so he resigned and joined Winchester House preparatory school in Northamptonshire. This gave him the opportunity to play for Leicester Tigers, making his debut in the 1929 season.

He was first picked for England three years later and in 1934 was made captain. He was the first Leicester Tiger to lead England. He was an outstanding scrum half who was 6ft 2 ins tall and of formidable build. It was said that besides being a ferocious tackler he was an early user of the reverse pass, propelling the ball at a tremendous pace. He won 14 international caps, captaining on eight occasions. Bernard led England to the Triple Crown in 1934, as well as captaining the Barbarians. Then in 1936 he led a British Lions tour to Argentina and they won all their ten games; in one, Prince Alexander Obolensky scored 17 tries.

Bernard Gadney also started the move for what is generally accepted to be the greatest try ever scored. From a scrum on England's 25 yard line he passed to Peter Candler, the outside half, who, two passes later, received it back from Peter Cranmer: Prince Alexander Obolensky, a Russian émigré, seeing no way down his right wing, darted inwards, took the pass from Candler and bolted through a gap and sprinted diagonally accross the pitch, a full seventy yards, scoring in the left corner'. This cemented England's first win against the mighty All Blacks. England winning by the margin of 13–0.

In the next decade for Leceister Tigers, he played 170 games, scoring 63 tries and 189 points and played his last game in 1938. In that year he moved to Malsis Preparatory school as Headmaster. Over the years he had remained friends with David Niven and both of them competed for the hand of Kelly Lilley of the Lilley and Skinner shoe family. Bernard won and the two were married. They went to France for their honeymoon, but had to beat a hasty retreat as war was declared.

With a new wife, at a new school on the edge of the Dales, in a reserved occupation (and suffering from asthma) nobody expected him to join the Navy as an Able Seaman he showed his true character. He rose through the ranks and was soon commissioned - one of his exploits was to take a landing craft accross the channel shortly after D-Day carrying armaments to his troops and returning with German POWs - After the war he returned to Malsis, originally he only had twelve boys, when he retired in 1960 he had 200.

When our man was recovering from five operations on his left knee, he saw an advertisement in the Daily Telegraph for the position of Cricket Coach at Malsis, he replied and was interviewed by Mr Gadney at the East India Club. He was offered and accepted the position. Bernard Gadney was a hard taskmaster, demanding all nine pitches were marked out each day BEFORE morning assembly, but against this chore, his curriculum was very supportive - coaching started at 9.30am and went on throughout the day, matches were on Wednesdays and Saturdays. His endeavour bore fruit as the first XI did not lose any matches. Sadly near the end of term he had to resign as he had to return to hospital for another operation. When Bernard retired, he and Kelly moved to Suffolk, where Bernard became a keen golfer. He also visited Obelinsky's grave, who had died in 1940 serving in the RAF.

Bernard Gadney was the first name to be inducted on to the Museum of Rugby's Wall of Fame with Nick Farr-Jones in November 2000, he should have unveiled the Wall, but sadly died a month prior to the launch.

David Turner

by Henriette Turner (*his wife*)

David Turner was born to Robert Edward and Peggy Turner on the 5th February 1949 in the small town of Corsham, Wiltshire.

David spent his childhood 'perfecting his craft' playing in the local Chippenham parks and fields. According to his peers, David was the only one who had any cricket equipment, and it was always the newest and latest equipment at that. David was well-known to the locals, asking the groundsman at John Coles Park to cut him a pitch to play on with his friends.

Of course, David was as serious and determined about the sport as he was in later years. This meant that he expected high standards from his team mates, and would often become irritated and leave when others failed to take it as seriously as he did.

At the age of 14 David was playing for Chippenham, where he scored his first century. By the age of 16, with the support and enthusiasm of his former headmaster, a cricket enthusiast, David began playing for Wiltshire in the school summer holidays. David maintains that the support of the head teacher and the high level of facilities at the school were a key feature in his success.

On leaving school at the age of 17, David was offered contracts with Somerset, Gloucester, Warwickshire and of course the club he spent the next 24 years with, Hampshire.

David, on moving to Hampshire at 17, was successful in the second team which earned him a debut first XI match against Kent at Bournemouth. It was unfortunate that David started with a duck in the first innings...but in his second innings scored 14 not out.

By the time he was 21 he was a fully capped player, after achieving 1000 runs in a season. He was already batting in the number three position; a position which he maintained for the majority of his career. In the later years, he also batted fairly regularly at the number five position.

In 1973, he went on the Derick Robbins Tour in South Africa, which was more or less an England A and B team. He returned the next year to play for Paarl Cricket Club where he managed to help the club to gain promotion to the Western League First Division. During his first season coaching and playing for Paarl Cricket Club he met his future wife, Henriette, who he eventually married in 1977, in the Paarl Dutch Reformed Church.

Over the next 11 years, David continued to play for Paarl, and the club maintained a very high standard; with the first team performing well in the first division.

In 1978, David was selected to play for the Western Province Currie Cup Team, in that season they won the championship.

In 1981, Hampshire Cricket Club awarded David a cricket benefit which consisted of fund-raising activities, dinners and functions. He also had several events organised by his friends from Chippenham, whom he had known since his early days playing cricket and football at school.

In 1984, during the Paarl cricket season, his wife Henriette gave birth to their first and only child, Nicola.

During his 24 year career (1966-1989) at Hampshire, David was in the winning teams for the John Player League on three separate occasions, the Benson and Hedges Cup at Lords, and the Hampshire County Cricket Club in 1973. David was the only Hampshire player ever to have been on the winning team for these three competitions. He is also the only Hampshire player to have played 24 consecutive seasons. In 1987, David was also voted as Hampshire County Cricket Club's Player of the Year.

On his retirement in 1989, David began working with his father in his home town of Chippenham in the family shoe business. David continued to play for Wiltshire Minor Counties as well as Chippenham Cricket Club. Eventually though, he turned his priorities to the business and turned his dedication to his new line of work. He did, however, continue to maintain his hand at cricket, playing for some of the local villages in friendly matches. Eventually though, rain stopped play, and David retired from cricket altogether. His last ever match played in the village of Biddestone in a friendly.

David has now exchanged his cricket bat for a golf club and manages to play in his spare time, at weekends and the odd evening. He continues to show the same determination and level of perfection in his golf and his work, as he did in all his years playing for Hampshire.

David continues to reside with his wife Henriette in Chippenham, working in the family shoe business, and enjoying his golf as a leisure pastime.

Desmond Eagar
(Gloucestershire and Hampshire CCCs)

By Patrick Eagar

Desmond Eagar's first first class innings came at the age of 17 when he played for Gloucestershire against Middlesex on the college ground at Cheltenham. It was doubly a home match for him, he was the College captain and had already played in the school XI for three years. He benefited from the advice of the College coach, "The first ball you receive will be a half volley outside the off stump, under no circumstances hit it for more than one". Those were the days – imagine the reception a 17-year-old schoolboy would receive today.

He was born in 1917, towards the end of the First World War. His father, a regular soldier, had been wounded four times in four years on the Western Front and was eventually taken prisoner by the Germans in early 1918. After the conclusion of hostilities the young Eagar travelled with his parents to various military postings including India and what was then Mesopotamia (now Iraq). His years at boarding schools encouraged his natural talent at many sports besides cricket and included hockey and rugby. He went up to Oxford and gained blues at hockey and cricket but never completed his degree as he joined the army in 1939. The war cost him a possible International hockey career for he had played a final England Trial in 1939.

In 1946, now aged 29, he answered an advertisement in *The Cricketer* magazine and applied for a job as Assistant Secretary and Captain of Hampshire. And there he stayed for the rest of his life.

His legacy as Hampshire captain was considerable. He inherited a side of pre-war professional cricketers and built a team that finished third in the County Championship in 1955, their highest ever position at that time. As a county cricketer he would be remembered for fielding close in on the leg side, either at leg slip or short leg. He took 369 catches in his career, most of them in this position. Batting lower down the order, he would craft an innings that was geared more to the needs of the team rather than his own personal average. He scored a thousand runs in a season five times for Hampshire. He also bowled (occasionally) slow left arm wrist spin.

As captain, there was always an element of local fame, and he may have been reluctant to give his autograph on every occasion. One day the cry went up, "Eagar's signing." A small boy scrambled forward and said, "Des, Des give me your autograph." The grumpy reply was instant, "Don't call me Des." "Why not?" was the repost, "the Daily Mirror does!"

Catches win matches, he would say, and whether masterminding schoolboy coaching classes or leading the county team he would insist on the highest fielding standards. It was a hall-mark of the team, and a strong basis from which Colin Ingleby-Mackenzie would lead them to their first ever County Championship title in 1961.

He went on tour to Australia with Peter May's ill-fated team in 1958-59. Known affectionately as "Cash" he was assistant manager to Freddie Brown. They had been billed as one of the strongest MCC teams ever to leave these shores but lost 4-0. The England batting line-up included Colin Cowdrey, Ted Dexter, Tom Graveney as well as Peter May and considering that the bowling included Frank Tyson, Brian Statham, Fred Trueman, Tony Lock and Jim Laker to name just a few, you wonder what could possibly go wrong?

He lived for cricket, especially Hampshire cricket. After his retirement from playing he immersed himself as administrator, historian, collector, commentator and journalist of the game he loved. He ran cricket in Hampshire negotiating the perils of government by committee with great skill. There always seemed a shortage of money, but through an intensive fostering of local talent nearly all the young players came from Hampshire (as well as some from the neighbouring counties of Wiltshire and Berkshire). At home matches, he could be found in the back office after the tea interval counting the cash from the day's gate. He would then personally bundle it up and deposit it in the local bank on his way home.

He was a cricket historian. In his spare time, he collected cricket books and built an exceptional library. He contributed to many books on cricket history, including the History of Hampshire Cricket with H S Altham, John Arlott and Roy Webber as co-authors (1957). One of his favourite projects was the annual publication, The Hampshire Handbook. He edited it (and wrote many articles for it) throughout his years with Hampshire.

His knowledge was appreciated by the MCC and for a long time he was a member of the Arts and Library Committee. When the Sunday Telegraph started up in 1961, he became their Hockey Correspondent in the winter months and was happy to write cricket reports whenever he had a spare Saturday in the summer.

He had been contemplating retirement in order to devote time to his other great love, stamp collecting. Sadly this never happened and he died suddenly while on holiday just a few months short of his sixtieth birthday.

Benjamin Gilbert Brocklehurst
b. 1922 – d. 2007

by Christopher Bazalgette

Ben was a very special gentleman. He was born at Knapton Hall in Norfolk, the son of a Canadian rancher. He was educated at Bradfield College, where he represented the school at football, tennis, squash and athletics and was captain of the Ist XI at cricket. He was Victor Ludorum at the Public Schools Sports held at the White City in 1938, winning both the Discus and the High Jump.

In the 2nd World War, he served initially in the 10th(Home Defense) Battalion of the Deveonshire Regiment. He was wounded in the Bristol blitz, and was commissioned into the Royal Berkshire Regiment. After which he transferred to the Indian Army, joining the Frontier Force Rifles. He was badly mauled by a bear in Kashmir and volunteered for service in Burma. On being promoted to Major, to command a Pashtun company in the 4th Battalion, a reconnaissance unit. He was later promoted to Lieutenant Colonel at the age of 24, taking control of two thousand Japanese prisoners of war. He was mentioned in Despatches.

On his return to England, he farmed for eight years at Finchampstead in Berkshire. He played cricket for Somerset in 1952/3/4, captaining them in 1953 and 1954. He played in 64 matches and scored 1671 runs, including six fifties. In a charity match against Hampshire he scored a double century. On his retirement from the first class game he played club cricket for MCC, I Zingari, Free Foresters, Arabs, Hampshire Hogs and The Bradfield Waifs. He was a very powerful hitter, but sadly played before the One-Day game started.

After farming he went into publishing, joining Country Life, later he moved to The Mercury House Group as Publishing Director, building a portfolio of seven trade and technical publications. After ten years he and his wife bought *The Cricketer* from the Company, this was in 1972.

His own title

In October of that year, the circulation was just under 12000 and advertisement revenue a shade over £10K, but his team were all professionals – E.W.(Jim)Swanton and Christopher Martin-Jenkins provided the editorial, Ben himself was the Ideas man, Harry Constantine was the Research man and Christopher Bazalgette was the salesman.

Ben decided the way to increase circulation was to organise cricket competitions, so those competing would take magazines.

The National Village Cricket Championship was first sponsored by Haig whisky, *The Cricketer* Cup for Public Schools Old Boy sides was sponsored by Moet & Chandon for 21 years and the Company Cup was sponsored by the Prudential Assurance.

The editorial team reported matches, conducted interviews and provided professional opinion.

At a later date the Company Cup was replaced by the National Colts Trophy for under 15's, with the Final played at Trent Bridge. This was funded by The Lord's Taverners (Ben was on the main Board) and arranged it in conjunction with ESCA.

David Frith was an early Editor, however, although an excellent writer, and extremely knowledgeable about cricket history, there was a clash of personalities and he left and started Wisden Cricket Monthly.

Reg Hayter became Editor and the circulation increased steadily (Reg ran an agency for sports journalists) and reached a peak of nearly 35,000 monthly. When he approached his 80th year, he resigned to be replaced by Christopher Martin-Jenkins, with Jim Swanton as Editorial Director.

Sponsorship and advertisement revenue had also taken off, Christopher almost reached £300,000, before it settled back to £280K per year. One of the main contributors to the increase was a feature he wrote every year was a 'World assessment of Cricket Equipment, Clothing and Footwear', this brought in some £50000 advertisement revenue.

The editorial content month-by-month was second to none, many readers would telephone if their magazine was even hours late. We also had overseas readers who regularly made pilgrimages to the Head Office, from all over the world.

Everything went very smoothly for twenty-eight years, the title had bought Playfair Cricket Monthly in 1973 and it became the leading cricket magazine throughout the world. The team had increased but the main operators were still in place. Sadly, Ben became very ill and the reigns passed to his son Tim. The old order were side lined and several changes were made. Computers were becoming more sophisticated, the Nationals introduced sports supplements and websites 'moved the goal posts'. Within four years the magazine was in decline, money was spent on a franchise (to bring more colour on board), sponsorships were lost and not replaced, with the outcome Paul Getty bought *The Cricketer* and Tim Brocklehurst, everybody else were made redundant. Wisden Cricket Monthly became The Wisden Cricketer, but only in title, little of *The Cricketer* could be seen in evidence.

I worked with Ben for forty two years, the first ten at Mercury House and thirty two years with *The Cricketer*. Ben was 'of the old school' he believed in hard honest toil, he looked after his staff and rewarded when he could, woe betide those who thought they could 'pull the wool over his eyes'.

My wife and I remember a wonderful week's holiday he

gave us on his motorised yacht sailing around the Ionian sea with her crew of boatmaster and chef, anchoring in small bays over night and picnicking on isolated beaches.

Every year the Final of the National Village Cricket Championship was held at Lords, in the first few years I used to run a 'Throwing the cricket ball competition' in the morning of the event. *The Cricketer* had a box and Ben invited both staff and celebrities to attend. Usually The President of MCC would visit together with people like Sir Len Hutton and Brian Johnston. The night before, each team plus wives and/or girl friends were accommodated at a nearby hotel and given a Dinner as part of the prize in reaching the Final.

Apart from his business success Ben was instrumental in running a holidays business. He also had a wonderful gift of being able to paint and draw to a high standard, many of his pictures portrayed the various holiday destinations at which guests could stay.

Ben was full of humour and loved hosting a party, he was well known for his generosity and kindness.

Ben died in 2007.

Arthur Holt

By Peter Haslop

Arthur Holt's all-round ability as a sportsman enabled him to become both a professional cricketer and a footballer. He made his debut for Southampton F.C. in 1934 and, as an inside forward, played more than 200 games, scored 46 goals and captained the side.

Holty made his debut for Hampshire in 1935, and in 78 matches he scored nearly 3,000 runs, including two centuries and ten fifties, before retiring as a player in 1948. His major contribution to cricket lay ahead of him, as coach – and that was how he was known until the day he died. Arthur was Hampshire's coach for 16 years and was also assistant to MCC's chief coach, Harry Crabtree. All the spade work for the first MCC coaching manual was provided by Holty himself.

He became a father figure to all the lads he coached and was much loved by all who had the privilege to have known him. His coaching took him to South Africa, Zimbabwe, South America, Ireland, Denmark, and Holland, where he coached their coaches. He was always approachable and always willing to listen and advise. Above all, he was one of nature's gentlemen, right to his death at the age of 83, always willing to assist club cricketers throughout Hampshire.

Even to this day, I still miss him so much. In the winter months he was out attending, and speaking, at cricket dinners; he even paid for his own dinner. He was Mr. Hampshire. We must not forget his wife Joan, for without her help and companionship, he would never have done what he did for the wonderful game of cricket, as he called it.

ED. Note: Arthur coached me from the time I was aged

eleven, in the years that followed I would telephone him on cricketing matters and through my life was always a guide to me. He invited me to join the Forty Club, after which I took his role of District Chairman and eventually joined the Executive Committee of the club.

Derek Shackleton

By Julian Shackleton

Derek Shackleton was born in Todmorden, Yorkshire, in August 1924, and educated at the local school, Roomfield. His father had played a few games for Lancashire Schools and then went on to play for Todmorden. When very young, my father contracted scarlet fever, which eventually damaged his left eye. As happens with kids, he did not tell his parents and it was only when the school advised them that they learnt of his problem.

When Derek was a teenager, he played in goal for Burnley F.C. and had a chance to join Stoke City. Instead, he was called up. He was keen to carry on with his football, which he played in the Army, but Hampshire's scouts asked him to go to Southampton for cricket trials. After discussions with his parents and his future wife, Kathy, he decided to sign for the club. Derek and Kathy were married in 1950 and I was born in 1952 in January, while father was on an MCC tour in India, Pakistan and Ceylon (now Sri Lanka). My sister Caroline was born two years later, both in Todmorden, of course, as our mother went home to ensure Yorkshire was the county on our birth certificates.

As a youngster growing up, I always remember dad being away a lot, but he used to bring me back Dinky cars and I still have a vivid memory of my sister sitting with him during the evening when he came home. Dad was always very smart and well turned out and taught my sister and me how to tie our shoes and clean them properly and how to tie a proper Windsor knot with our school ties.

Derek Shackleton's cricketing exploits are well documented. I spent hours at Northlands Road, Southampton, watching and playing cricket behind the stands with crowds of kids. My first realisation of how good he was came during a match at Portsmouth, when, in the tea interval, we went out to the pitch and examined the end to which Dad had been bowling for most of the day. There was a bare patch measuring about 8 x 10 inches on which he kept pitching the ball.

I know he was surprised and excited about playing against West Indies in 1963. He had a lot of respect for Sir Frank Worrell, their captain. I went to the Oval to watch that Test match and thoroughly enjoyed the experience. I knew then what I wanted to do for a career.

Although dad was away at cricket a lot, at heart he was a home bird, wanting to be with mum and his children. He was not a great socialiser, although he knew how to enjoy himself when he had to attend functions. He was very fortunate that Hampshire awarded him two benefits. Had it not been for the second one, we might have emigrated to New Zealand as he had been offered a couple of coaching posts there.

After his cricket career finished, he coached at Canford School, in Wimborne, and the family moved to Ferndown. Derek had a short spell as a first-class umpire, which he thoroughly enjoyed for four years and was very upset when that came to an end.

He returned to Canford, where by now his wife had started running the school shop, which she did for 26 years.

By the time dad retired, his sight was slowly deteriorating and his bad eye went blind. In the next ten to 15 years he gradually lost sight in the other eye. After my mother's death in 2004, he went downhill and developed Alzheimers, which he suffered at home until his death in 2007. He now rests in peace with his wife Kathy up on the moors above Todmorden.

CHAPTER 2

First Honours

Beyond ones wildest dreams!

1977 marked the Bi-Centenary of Hambledon playing All England – between 1771 and 1793 this match had been played 51 times and Hambledon had won 29 of them – MCC would represent All England.

Already a member of the Hambledon CC and known for his promotional skills, Christopher was asked to help the committee putting on the event, subsequently his marketing plan was adopted and he found the sponsor. He was invited and accepted the opportunity to play. The occasion was a huge success, he bowled a maiden over to Sir Colin Cowdrey, who bowled the last ball and had our man stumped and the match was a draw.

He was given the honour of being made an Honorary Life member, in time he was joined by first David Gower, then Topsy Turner – a living legend who had scored the most runs and taken the most wickets for all time for the club, as well as being a fantastic club member; plus latterly a former club Hon. Secretary and benefactor Ron Turner has made up the quartet. The Club Captain was Colin Barrett, who also arranged fixtures, was groundsman and was an allround cricketer in every sense of the word, he could bat aggressively, save a batting collapse, bowl slow spinners, medium pace and was one of the greatest captains Christopher ever played with or against. Christopher represented Hambledon in the 'Down your way' programme meeting Brian Johnston and discussing cricket on Broadhalfpenny Down.

The Cricketer was gathering pace and took most of his time, alongside these activities, his own reputation was growing and prior to the New Zealand team's tour to UK (1978), he was asked to help with the commercial support for the tour. This development included the production of the tour brochure that was achieved in ten days and brought him in direct contact with the team, who were captained by Simon Burgess. As they needed some warm up practice it was agreed they should play a match against The Hampshire Hogs, so it was not surprising for our man to arrange the sponsorship, as well as playing in the match. Their full side attended the game including Richard Hadlee, who later was knighted and was recognised as one of the leading opening bowlers of all time, besides being no mean allrounder.

Our man was not out and the Match was reported as a draw in the tour report. He was invited to many of the tour's matches and events, at the end of their tour in England a cocktail party was held on top floor of New Zealand House, during the evening the Captain asked one of the players – Bev Congdon, to remove his tour tie and present it to him.

1979 was a very special year, for one of the promotion agents he visited advised him that they could find some £70000 from one of their clients, who wished to sponsor a cricket competition, but it had to be special.

A friend of his, Roger Thompson had mounted a head to head between Barry Richards and Viv Richards on the Somerset ground at Taunton, one of the pre-runners of single wicket matches in England. Together they dreamed up a new format, they planned to asked the eight best batsmen in the world to play a single wicket competition, but with a twist, there would be eight of the best fast bowlers, four medium pace bowlers and four spinners, plus two of the best wicket-keepers, the venue was the Kennington Oval, so the Surrey County side acted as the fielders and four of the leading umpires adjudicated. The current England Captain, Mike Brearley chose the players. The sponsor was Courage, the event was called 'The International Batsman of the Year' for The Courage Challenge Cup. The prize was £5000 and the event cost £100,000.

Publicity was vital, one hundred and forty six papers and magazines carried details prior to and following the two-day occasion and regular TV coverage was gained on BBC sport, due to the foresight of Cliff Morgan who was responsible for outside broadcasts. Clive Lloyd beat David Gower in the final. This was Christopher's first major sponsorship.

In cricketing terms this event was a seriously great occasion.

For many years he was a member of The Hampshire County Cricket Club and now he was to become involved with their beneficiaries, the first was Richard Gilliatt, by arranging with the beneficiary to play the Hogs, it was his responsibility to find a sponsor and create a promotional brochure, thus making money for both sides and a worthwhile venture.

In 1979 it was the turn of Barry Richards, whose friendship with the Hughes family, who in turn, were great stalwarts of the Hampshire Hogs, together they arranged for the County to play the Club to support Barry's benefit. The game was sponsored and various marketing methods enabled both principals to gain satisfactory returns from the initiative. His next beneficiary he was to help was David Turner, this time he was on the benefit committee, David brought his County team-mates to play the Hogs and our man led the marketing operation, he also played in the match and travelled with Hampshire when they flew to Alderney, Guernsey and Jersey as part of the perks for the benefit work. He was unaware that it was to become very close to a 'Lost' weekend. For the only way each island was able to compete, was to attempt to make each Hampshire player completely legless prior to the match. For the Alderney game we changed in a large marquee, luckily mobile phones did not take photographs then, as several players found it hard to realise in which holes legs and arms should go, the remainder were creased with laughter at their antics. As the game was played on top of a hill and we had some big hitters, they only had just enough balls to complete the match, which was enjoyed immensely by all who participated.

Later there was another party, which was invaded by some not invited guests, so a hasty getaway was embarked upon. However, there was only two cars, maybe you can allow your imagination to encompass how you squeeze fourteen fit large men into two medium size cars, it was decided to take the coast road so the charade was not witnessed.

The next day we moved to Guernsey, more serious cricket but still in festival mode, rather than staying in a hotel everybody was billeted in people's homes. The Captain and our man had the privilege of staying with Brigadier Mike White and his family, whose home was on the north west coast of the island. Mike was an institution, already in his seventies he had a net in the garden and still played regular cricket, by the bedside was the latest issue of *The Cricketer* and the current Wisden. Nobody could have been more welcoming and his wife treated their guests as if all had known each other for years. We were all sorry to move to the more commercial Jersey, we had to fly back to Alderney before returning to Hampshire.

Alderney was the home of the celebrated commentator John Arlott, to where he had retreated with his wonderful collection of wines and his books, another celebration those still capable were able to enjoy, John was a wonderful host and together with numerous anecdotes made this day very special.

The Islander aircraft carried sixteen people inclusive of the pilot, quite intimate and fairly basic, this transport was enjoyable to the majority but abhorrent to the Captain, one Nick Pocock, who wished to sit at the back with eyes firmly closed, when we took off. As the plane circled the aerodrome before heading back to Southampton, it was realised there was an empty seat which explained the figure madly waving his arms on the runway. The Captain – NEP was informed and he said 'Leave him, he should have been on time' or words to that effect, the pilot was a compassionate man and said he would go back for the fellow. So poor Nick had to endure more landings and take-offs, amongst great hilarity.

One opportunity that arose in 1980 will stand out as the best occasion in this man's life, it was never confirmed who orchestrated it, but an invitation arrived for him to meet the Old Australians who had been invited for the Centenary of England v. Australia, this took place at The Russell Hotel on 21st August 1980. Only seventeen Englishmen attended and he was one. All the Australians lined up and everybody shook hands and was introduced. Our man's heroes on both sides: Australians - Ray Steele, Ray Walsh, Bill O'Reilly, Bill Johnstone, Neil Harvey, Keith Miller, Ray Lindwall, Lindsay Hassett, Jim De Courcy, Colin McDonald, Ernie Toshack, Don Tallon and Arthur Morris. Their English counterparts included Colin Cowdrey, Jim Laker, Ted Dexter, Tony Lock, Peter Loader and Alec Bedser. The doyen of cricket writing Reg Hayter, represented the press, Peter Lush, representing the National Board. After a while small groups moved to the bar and our man was with Neil Harvey, Ray Lindwall, Keith Miller, Don Tallon, Ernie Toshack and Colin McDonald and Peter Lush. When it came near his round he had a dilemma, for earlier in the day he had been taken out to lunch, but he had to pay, so now he was short of funds. Afterwards he was meeting someone across London with whom he was staying the night. It was a case of the cost of the taxi or the round of drinks. This he chose, after which he had to take his leave. He found a taxi and explained his situation and the taxi driver said 'Have this one on me', so ended a perfect day. Several times during the evening he pinched himself to convince him it wasn't just a dream.

Brian Johnston

By Andrew Johnston

Brian Johnston was known as 'Johnners' to millions of cricket fans around the world. For nearly 50 years he was the voice of cricket on BBC television and radio. When Brian died in 1994 at the age of 81, the Daily Telegraph described him as 'the greatest natural broadcaster of them all' and the British Prime Minister, John Major, appeared to speak for the nation when he said: 'Summers will never be the same.'

Brian was born at Little Berkhamsted, Hertfordshire, the youngest of four children, on June 24, 1912. His father ran the Johnston family coffee business in the City of London and his grandfather was a Governor of the Bank of England. Brian was educated at Eton and New College, Oxford. He wanted to be an actor but he was persuaded to enter the family coffee business instead. When war was declared in 1939 he joined the 2nd Battalion Grenadier Guards, where he served as a Technical Adjutant and was awarded the Military Cross.

In January 1946 Brian joined the BBC. He only planned to stay for a few months but he was to work for the BBC for the next 48 years. His first broadcasts were live radio programmes from music-halls and theatres around the country. He began his cricket commentating career at Lord's for BBC Television in June 1946 at the England v India Test match and he was one of the first broadcasters to work for both television and radio. Between 1948 and 1952 he made his name with the live feature Let's Go Somewhere on the popular Saturday night radio programme In Town Tonight. In these early years, Brian was an occasional presenter of other BBC shows, including Come Dancing and All Your Own. Among his 150 stunts, Brian stayed alone in the Chamber of Horrors, rode a circus horse, lay under a passing train, was hauled out of the sea by a helicopter and was attacked by a police dog.

In 1948 Brian Johnston married Pauline Tozer, formerly of Sheffield. They had five children. In the 'fifties and 'sixties he presented children's television shows such as All Your Own, Ask Your Dad and What's New, while on radio he interviewed hundreds of personalities on Today, Meet a Sportsman, Married to Fame and many other series. He also broadcast from the Boat Race for 42 years.

Brian appeared on dozens of quiz shows and panel games including Sporting Chance, Twenty Questions and Trivia Test Match, and commentated on all the major state occasions such as the funeral of King George VI, the Coronation and the wedding of the Prince and Princess of Wales. He officially retired from the BBC in 1972 but then he turned freelance and presented the radio series Down Your Way for the next 15 years.

Finally, of course, Brian was a cricket commentator on television from 1946 and became the BBC's first cricket correspondent in 1963. After he was dropped by television for being too humorous, Brian transferred to radio in 1970, where he became a national institution on Test Match Special. From 1972 to 1987, Brian Johnston presented Down Your Way on BBC Radio Four, in which he visited a different city, town or village, interviewing local figures (not necessarily celebrities) and playing a piece of music selected by them at the end of each interview.

At the age of 80 Brian achieved a lifelong ambition with his one-man show, An Evening with Johnners, in which he told his hilarious anecdotes and jokes to sell-out audiences around the country. The CD became the best selling spoken word recording in the UK and even entered the pop album charts.

After Brian's death on January 5 1994, his memorial service

was held at a packed Westminster Abbey in May. More than 2,000 people were present.

His widow, Pauline, subsequently founded the Brian Johnston Memorial Trust, a charity which awards annual Brian Johnston Scholarships to promising young cricketers in need of financial support and also helps to sponsor cricket for the blind.

The author writes

Brian Johnston was the total professional. I remember on one occasion we were having drinks prior to lunch at the National Village Championship final at Lord's. Johners and Pauline, his wife, were there and he remarked that he had to put a piece on tape for the lunchtime news, so would go to the front of the box only a few rows away from the guests.

The professional switched from lighthearted chatter to the recording. Fifteen minutes elapsed. Brian, with only a few notes, had spoken continuously and then in the same detached way, switched back to being the conversationalist.

Brian's strength was his ease of talking, whether with celebrities and friends from all walks of life, or describing the environment or event developing in front of him. He was a natural, he possessed charm, kindness, bags of humour interwoven with a mischievous twinkle of his eye. One of his trademarks was his method of written communication: Naughty postcards! with double entendre.

Every day he watched 'Neighbours' and then would telephone his great friend, Sir Paul Getty, to discuss the finer points...

After his formal funeral the family asked that the final music the Westminster Abbey organ played would be the theme tune from *Neighbours*. The Dean agreed.

Michael Colin Cowdrey,
Baron Cowdrey of Tonbridge CBE

By Christopher Cowdrey

Colin Cowdrey's most endearing quality was simply that he had 'time'- time for anyone, anytime - and of course time to play the ball.

I remember him driving 30 minutes out of his way to deliver cup final tickets to a gateman from St. Lawrence Ground, Canterbury. 'I don't think I can risk the post and I would hate him to miss the game!' He almost saw it as his duty as captain of Kent.

I recall the day when I hopped into the back of my father's car for the first day of a Championship match at Maidstone. We were very late - we were always late because he had normally been on the phone on England business before we could leave for a county cricket match. Worse still on this occasion we were caught in a traffic jam and there were no mobile phones back in the late 'sixties - or motorways for that matter.

A short cut through the Kent farm lanes offered a loose herd of cattle and a diversion sign that led to nowhere. With the match starting in under an hour in Maidstone, we came across a village cricket ground where there was an under-11's match taking place. This was the perfect opportunity to borrow the club phone box to call Brian Luckhurst, the Kent vice-captain that day, to give him the team and get him to toss the coin in his absence. 'Try to bat first, Lucky, The Mote is always a good pitch!'

Can you imagine the excitement on the village green when the Kent and England skipper arrived at their pavilion door? Especially as he was in his whites all ready for action (he often arrived for county matches changed, with training before the game never on the agenda).

Phone call and signatures completed, he became fascinated by a little leg spinner being slogged into the field by a much bigger boy. For the next 20 minutes (getting later all the time for his county match) he chatted to the young boy as he walked disconsolately down to fine leg after another expensive over. He encouraged him to keep giving the ball some air to gain his rewards. Eventually the skyer went up and an unlikely hero hung on to the catch. M.C.Cowdrey jumped up and down like a nine year-old. The boy had no idea who he was and as we hurried off to the car, the youngster with a Cheshire cat grin cried out to the England captain, "Thanks Mate!"

Forty minutes later he was batting at number four at The Mote for Kent.

An undying memory of growing up as a child, as son of the England cricket captain, was of the endless phone calls that would interrupt his few precious moments at home. Selectors, well wishers, team mates, but more often than not, the media; and even more often than not John Thicknesse of the *Evening Standard*. He was a menace, sounding full of scotch and desperate to extract a snippet of information for his article: the word 'no' was unacceptable to him. Why should Colin Cowdrey eat his dinner without interruption, when I have a piece to submit? Sadly, my father never said 'no' to anyone and family and friends pleaded with him endlessly to be more selfish with his time. He couldn't do it despite the warnings that one day it would be the end of him. Colin Cowdrey felt that he had come from a relatively privileged background although several years growing up on his own away from his parents had been quite a hardship; simply he treated everyone in life from his friend on the Canterbury gate to royalty with utmost respect. Even a life peerage never changed him.

He would always sign autographs for ages after a long day's

play; he would always try to answer letters from supporters or antagonists; he would always speak at charity events or open the church fete; he would always take a phone call - he never said 'no' and eventually it did kill him.

As a cricketer, I suppose there was an element to his style of batting that fitted into the genius bracket. Was there ever a player who timed a cover drive better than M.C.Cowdrey? It was a freakish touch that he couldn't coach - I mean look at me. For hours he would explain how easy it was to hit a length ball outside off stump past cover point's right hand without him really noticing. I never managed it!

This is how he did it. Firstly, he would pick out an advertising board in between cover point and extra cover - this was the target - ideally there would be a word on the board to focus his mind further. Secondly, he would relax his bottom hand on the grip because it is 'only there to steer the ball' on its course. Thirdly, waiting till the ball was almost past him, he would quietly move his whole body like rocking a baby in a cradle through the line of the ball, (which should now be passing under his nose).

Fourthly, he would remind his bottom hand to take aim and with a bit of luck 'you really should be able to pick out the board, you know.' Genius!

He loved his cricket and believed that he should give everything back to the game that had been so good to him. He did this through various roles, as president of MCC and the first ICC Chairman. But it was his creation of the 'Spirit of Cricket' with Ted Dexter at his side that is perhaps his legacy. He was concerned for the future of the game in the mid-'nineties and was determined to achieve the implementation of the 'Spirit of Cricket' into the Laws of Cricket. He was fearful of player behaviour undermining umpires and setting poor standards for children, which is perhaps the downside of contact sports like football. I am sure he will look down on our game and believe that gradually the world is buying into the 'Spirit of Cricket.' One day it will be recognised as the addition to the Laws that kept the game in good shape for – perhaps - another century.

For me and my brother Graham, it wasn't always easy following a father of such eminence into cricket; yet he had few enemies in the game and generally we were welcomed by most players and administrators around the world with open arms. So many people, so many friends with so much to thank him for and we were the lucky beneficiaries. However, there is always one!

In my case it was a guy called Ken Higgs. As I started out in county cricket he was coming to the end of a second career with Leicestershire. As an aggressive fast medium bowler, it rather suited him to have someone like me on whom to release his anger and bitterness. The gist of what he told me in language not printable was that my father had unreasonably left him out of an England team many years before.

Ken abused me on and off the field at every opportunity, always contravening the 'Spirit of Cricket.' In 1978, when Ray Illingworth set Kent 286 to win in about 50 overs at Grace Road, it was fun for me, batting with Graham Johnson, to smack Ken all over the place to win the game. The story should have amused my father; perhaps it did somewhere deep down, but his only offering was simply, 'he was a fine bowler, Ken Higgs!'

The 'old man' was a committed parent without having the luxury of much time to spend at home. Six month tours away, long county seasons, and rarely a Christmas by the fire with his family. It is sad he didn't have more time to have watched his many grandchildren trying to pick out that advertising board. A time when he could have been an armchair critic and a time when he might have rested for once, for the good of Colin Cowdrey.

Sir Richard John Hadlee

Canterbury, Nottinghamshire, Tasmania, New Zealand

By Michael Dormer

Richard Hadlee was a young tearaway fast bowler in his early years with Canterbury from his long flowing locks to his inconsistent bowling which varied from game to game and innings to innings.

On some days he lacked aggression, fire and control. After his eighth test in three years he had taken 21 wickets at an average of 41.61.

His ninth Test was against India at the Basin Reserve in February 1976. Suddenly all the tiny facets that contribute to a bowler's action were working in perfect unison. In the second innings he became an imperious figure. His run up was fluid, his delivery, a graceful, sweeping motion. His figures of 7-23 in the second innings and his match analysis of 11-58 were both New Zealand test records. It was New Zealand's ninth Test victory and its first by an innings.

Two years elapsed before Hadlee played his next Test at the Basin, but in that time his batting was developing. He became a formidable lower order left-hand batsman who excelled at hitting quick bowlers from Pakistan and Australia over the fence. The greatest improvement in his cricket came with his maturing attitude and his increased heart.

Against England in February 1978 Richard Hadlee was the pivotal figure in New Zealand's ever improving status in Test cricket. In a low scoring game, New Zealand beat England for the first time in 46 years, over 48 games. Hadlee's analysis of 10-100 was the match winner. Later that year Hadlee began his association with Nottinghamshire and he realised that to extend his career it was imperative that he reduce his lengthy run-up.

His ever improving batting saw the cricket world press forever pushing the claims of the four great all-rounders, Ian Botham, Kapil Dev, Imran Khan and Richard Hadlee, and the rivalry between these super cricketers drew crowds to Tests. Playing for Nottinghamshire in 1984 he completed the double of 1,000 runs and 100 wickets in the season.

Perhaps the greatest ten months in his illustrious career began on 8 November 1985 at Brisbane and ended at The Oval against England on 26 August 1986. At the age of 34 he created Test records at a breathtaking pace. Beginning in Brisbane he captured nine Australian wickets in the first innings and six in the second. In the three Tests in Australia, New Zealand won two and lost one. He captured 33 wickets in the three tests. This had only been bettered once in a three test series, and that was by George Lohmann for England against South Africa on uncovered wickets in 1895-96.

His domination of the Australian batsmen continued in New Zealand where he captured a further 16 wickets. In three Tests in England he captured a further 19 wickets, giving him a total of 68 wickets in 9 Tests, at the remarkable low average of 17.32. New Zealand won the three series involved. It was the first time they had beaten Australia in Australia and England in England.

When he retired aged 39 he had taken the most Test wickets, 431, taken the most five-wicket bags, 36, and taken the most 10 wickets in a match, 9 times. His statistics point to Richard Hadlee being the greatest bowler of his type in the history of the game.

In 1990 he became a Knight Bachelor for his services to cricket and in 2000 he was named the New Zealand Sportsman of the Decade, 1980 – 89, at the Halberg Awards. After being the chairman of the New Zealand selectors he was made a Life Member of New Zealand Cricket.

Richard is very much a family man residing in Christchurch

with his wife Dianne where they are able to pursue a number of interests outside of cricket.

Regretfully, Richard lost both his Mother and his Father within the last two years. His Father, Walter, was the Captain of the New Zealand 1949 touring team to the UK and is well recognised as the doyen of New Zealand Cricket.

Test batting and fielding

P	I	NO	Runs	HS	Ave	100	50	Ct.
86	134	19	3,124	151	27.16	2	15	39

Test bowling

Balls	Runs	Wkts	Ave	5WI	10WM
21,918	9,611	431	22.29	36	9

First-class batting and fielding

P	I	NO	Runs	HS	Ave	100	50	Ct.
342	473	93	12,052	210*	31.71	14	59	198

First-class bowling

Balls	Runs	Wkts	Ave	5WI	10WM
-	26,998	1,490	18.11	102	18

Michael Edward Francis Dormer

By Don Neely

Upon meeting Michael Dormer for the first time 56 years ago, I was told that he played rugby and cricket and I knew immediately which positions he played in – scrum half and wicket-keeper. He was diminutively solid of build and had, and still has to this day, penetrative eyes that never leave you in the course of a discussion. He remains focussed on the person with whom he is conversing.

As a team-mate in the Wellington u-20 representative team, I saw that he was neat in style and demeanour and had been well trained by the coach of the Nelson College first XI, Graham Botting. He was nimble on his feet and stood up to the stumps to all but the fastest bowlers. His soft hands enabled him to effect stumpings off wayward medium-paced bowlers straying down the leg side.

He later played four first-class games for Auckland in 1961-62, holding five catches and taking three stumpings. Before that, he played mid-week cricket for the Wellington Wanderers against local colleges. He observed that his older team mates talked to their opponents, offering them coaching tips during the match. These coaching lessons continued after the game, encouraged by the appreciative lads who were seeking further information.

Whilst working in the United Kingdom in the mid-'sixties, he played regularly for the London New Zealand Cricket Club. These games exposed him to the beautiful grounds in England and the manner in which the games were played, as well as illustrating the courtesy that players showed towards their opponents and the traditions of the game. Playing for I Zingari, in and around Sydney in the 'seventies, he again conveyed his cricket knowledge to eager youngsters.

When his two boys, Peter and Ben, began to play sport, their father took a keen interest in the games and became immersed in their organisation. Little did he realise that all his first 30 years were but a progression towards creating a unique cricket club. For in 1993, Michael's wife, Winsome, bought a small farm, 9.4 kms from Rangiora, at Loburn, North Canterbury, mainly for the existing old cob cottage. Wandering over the cow paddock, Ben convinced Michael that it would make an excellent cricket ground.

Michael invited several friends to visit the farm and have a picnic with their family, feed the ducks and collect pine cones as well as seeking their opinions about forming a cricket club. They concurred and became loyal disciples. In spite of Winsome informing him he was 'mad,' creating a cricket ground became Michael Dormer's consuming passion.

A committee of 12 agreed on a suitable name, 'The Willows,' and their objectives,

- To encourage players at secondary school first XI standard to play with and against experienced players, many of whom would be past and present first-class cricketers.
- To offer quality cricket to cricket lovers in a country atmosphere, where families come to watch and picnic.

Working at a frenetic pace a cricket square (wicket block) was prepared,

A pavilion built with bat and wicket balustrade and a replica of the Father Time weather vane at Lord's sat atop a clock. Roses were planted at the side of the structure.

The 'great old man' of New Zealand cricket, Walter Hadlee was asked to be the Patron and readily agreed and expressed amazement as to what was happening at Loburn. On October

24th 1994, the Patron cut the ceremonial ribbon, declaring the club and season open. Both the vicar of Rangiora and the Rector of St. Bede's College blessed the Club. The first of twelve games was started with The Willows team including three former Test and two current first-class cricketers.

The attractive pavilion walls were covered with photographs of former cricketers, the score box, sightscreens, maintenance sheds, separate coaching and practice area, plus swings and slides for toddlers were all in position thanks to the dynamism, vision and generosity of one man – Michael Dormer. He had created a cricket field of his dreams.

The club has steadily grown in stature and is well known throughout New Zealand and wherever New Zealand cricket is talked about. The views and tranquil setting has seen some of New Zealand finest cricketers as visitors including The Governor General of New Zealand, His Excellancy Sir Anand Satyanand who brings his youth XI. Every two years they have a dinner for over 130 diners.

Every year the club publish an annual yearbook which covers the new horizons to which the members have reached out, they also include many friends from around the world – many of whom they make Honorary members. Some have toured from overseas with teams others made single pilgrimages.

A note from the Author: (Hon. member of Willows CC)

Michael Dormer welcomes all visitors to South Island New Zealand, he is the most generous and supportive host you can possibly find, always dedicating both himself and his wife, Winsome, to making new friends, remembering old friends and caring for the youth of tomorrow. There is no finer ambassador for cricket, some endeavour to follow in his wake, but if there were more Michael Dormers around the world, this planet would be a better place.

Brigadier William Michael Eastwood White
OBE

By Ann White (*his wife*)

When his father came to see his baby in Barnes in 1913, the doctor said it was too small and blue and would be best if it didn't live. Michael survived, however, although he was very short sighted, and initially he was taught to bat and bowl by his mother. His cricket progressed quickly when he went to school in Dover after the family had moved away from London. His other great love, emanating from that, was sea fishing. Every fish caught was carefully recorded.

He won a scholarship to Cambridge – going to Trinity Hall (in error, because his mother thought that was where her father had been). In fact he had been to Trinity College. Mike intended to read mathematics but decided zoology was more his metier – simply because of his love for fishing, He gained his degree in 1937 and taught briefly at Portsmouth Grammar School. He failed to land a job at one of the schools he had chosen and so decided to join the Army. Although he played eight first-class matches for Cambridge, he failed to gain a Blue, being pipped by Norman Yardley. He was commissioned in the Royal Army Service Corps and was posted to France in 1939, but in 1940 was evacuated as he developed jaundice just prior to Dunkirk (his replacement spent five years as a POW). Following service in North Africa and Italy, he was 'Mentioned in Dispatches' and awarded an OBE (Mil) in 1944. He still managed to fit in eight matches for the British Empire XI in 1941 and subsequently played at such unlikely venues as a Tunisian hillside and a Roman sports stadium.

After hostilities his performances for Army and Combined Services teams attracted the attention of Northamptonshire and in 1947 he celebrated his county debut with spells of three wickets in six balls in each of Somerset's innings. The feat that gave him most pleasure was achieved in July 1949 when he scored two separate hundreds in the day, the second of which carried the Aldershot Services to victory over MCC. In 21 first-class matches he scored 398 runs and took 42 wickets.

Promoted to Brigadier in 1959, his post-war roles included becoming commandant of the RASC Training Centre and Director of Supplies and Transport - Far East Land Forces. After six years (1963-69) as aide-de-camp to the Queen, during which he was appointed CBE, he retired to Guernsey to indulge in cricket, golf and fishing.

In addition to serving as president of Guernsey Island CC and the illustrious Incogniti CC from 1972 to 1983, he also became Commodore of the Royal Channel Isles Yacht Club. At 72 he finally hung up his cricket boots after heading the Island CC bowling averages. His final public appearance was to watch his daughter Julia make her cricketing debut for the Guernsey Sirens.

Barry Richards

By Bill Hughes

Any cricketer's sporting life will be influenced and enhanced by watching first hand the skills and abilities of an international cricketer who dominated his era. Barry Richards was that influence on me. I was one of the fortunate Hampshire members who enjoyed some remarkable displays of batting. Barry and his opening partner, Gordon Greenidge, were an integral part of the success that Hampshire enjoyed through the late 1960s and 1970s, culminating in them winning the County Championship in 1973.

Limited international exposure due to the exclusion of South Africa from Test cricket allowed all those who supported or watched Hampshire through that era to experience watching one of the greatest batsmen to grace the cricket arena. Who can forget the arrogant demolition of some of the finest attacks in the modern game? It was almost with disdain (and sometimes boredom) that Barry played some of his finest innings. Perhaps one of the most extraordinary was his 325 not out in November 1970 for South Australia against a Western Australia attack of Dennis Lillee, Graeme McKenzie and Tony Lock, which was exceptional. In a tribute to Barry from the great Sir Donald Bradman for Barry's benefit brochure in 1977, he said, "Sadly, one reflects on the words used by Wisden: 'Richards' horizons seem limitless and it will be fascinating to see how far his talents will take him'.

International politics denied Barry the opportunity of producing the records in the Test match arenas which undoubtedly would have placed him in the highest bracket with a batting average over 55. It is one of the great tragedies of today's world that enormous personal skill must be sacrificed on the altar of a principle."

His achievements for Hampshire, Natal, South Africa, Transvaal and World Series Cricket speak for themselves. He averaged more than 72 in his severely limited four Test career, and 54 at first-class level. He was one of the few batsmen in the world who could change the destination of a Hampshire supporter if he was not out overnight at Northlands Road. Somehow that appointment or meeting scheduled for 11.30 am was always rescheduled or postponed! A Richards /Greenidge partnership was an amazing experience that left the spectator with both a warm feeling of satisfaction and disappointment that it did not last longer.

Barry became a strong friend of Hampshire cricket in spite of a difficult departure from the county. This friendship culminated in his election as president of Hampshire in 2008 at their new home at the Rose Bowl. His skill and experience on the field of play transferred with the same ease as he had shown at the crease to broadcasting and cricket punditry, his opinion greatly respected by all viewers and listeners.

The last word on Barry's impact on the cricket world must go to Bradman, who chose him as one of the opening batsmen in his twentieth century team. This accolade after just four Test Matches! We Hampshire folk will always claim Barry as a Hampshire man and cricketer but he will be remembered to the whole cricketing world as one of the great talents whose Test career, alas, was unfulfilled.

Reg Hayter

by Peter Hayter

At the time of Reg Hayter's passing, aged 80, on March 13, 1994, the England cricket team was preparing to play a Test match against West Indies in Georgetown, Guyana, and the travelling press corps were preparing to write about it.

The sense of loss was felt as deeply within the England dressing room as it was in the press box.

England's opening bowler, Angus Fraser, had known Reg almost all his cricketing life, as he grew up playing for Reg's beloved Stanmore CC and even more beloved social team Elvino's. Among the scribblers present to report on his performance, no fewer than four had trained at Reg's Fleet Street sports reporting agency, Hayters' – Alan Lee of The *Times*, John Thicknesse of the *Evening Standard*, Chris Lander of *The Mirror* and John Etheridge of *The Sun*. A fifth, Peter Hayter of The *Mail On Sunday*, had tried, in vain, to return home in time to say goodbye.

No wonder when the Cricket Writers' Club pondered a suitable tribute to be inscribed on the blue plaque that bears his name in the press box at Lord's, they chose the following : Reg Hayter, who loved the game, the players and the writers.

Nor was cricket the only sport to enjoy his attentions. From the day he founded the agency in 1955, Reg trained stringers and staff men to write and broadcast about all of them for newspapers, books, radio and television. It is a fair bet that once his trainees started going out into the world to fend for themselves, a Hayters man was read by someone somewhere every day, and still is being, for, at the time of writing Peter is still the cricket correspondent of the *Mail On Sunday*, Etheridge still shines in The Sun, Alan Lee is now the racing correspondent of The Times, Rob Kitson is The Guardian's rugby man, Martin Samuel is the chief sports writer for the Daily Mail, Steve Ryder presents live football for ITV, as does Richard Keys for Sky.

And a sample from the list of those sportsmen who called him friend and adviser as well as agent is even more impressive: Denis Compton, Bill Edrich, Keith Miller, Alec Bedser, Godfrey Evans, Basil D'Oliveira, Tony Greig, Ray Illingworth. Ian Botham, Henry Cooper, Malcolm Macdonald...

Reg would far rather have been a player himself. Born in Paddington in 1913, four years earlier than his wife, Lucy, who was to bear him five children, in his youth his goal-scoring exploits for Ealing Dean prompted a local paper reporter to comment: "It is rumoured that only a brick wall could stop him."

As a genuinely quick and unerringly accurate pace bowler, he was known to have broken stumps and was employed as a net bowler by England on more than one overseas tour.

But his future was settled when, after matriculating from Marylebone Grammar School at the turn of the 1930s, he applied for, and got, a job with Pardon's Agency, and, on his first day as a reporter picked up a ringing telephone to find Herbert Chapman, the manager of Arsenal, on the other end.

Chapman was the biggest non-playing name in football at the time and his side were the greatest footballing force in the land. Hayter was a new boy with a pronounced stammer. It could have been carnage. Chapman instead put the youngster immediately at ease: "Reg - (he even called him Reg). I'm manager of Arsenal seven days a week, 365 days a year. Call me any time you want and write what you like – but don't ignore us."

Sixty years in Fleet Street later, the 80 year-old who had seen and done everything in sports journalism told that story with the same wide-eyed wonder as he did the first time round.

After the War, Reg was appointed the chief cricket correspondent for the Press Association, loaned out to Reuters on England's overseas tours, and it was in this role, in South Africa, Australia and West Indies that he forged the trusted relationships with players that enabled him to leave the PA and set up his own business.

The worst winter on record promptly made him and Lucy, who did the accounts in those early days, seriously question the decision as no sport meant precious little income, but, as he had already perfected the eight-day working week and the 25-hour day, it was only matter of time and clear skies before his enthusiasm and energy drove the business through the crisis and beyond.

Successive generations of sports editors were to fall under the spell of his friendship, a tincture or two and a constant stream of ideas of news, features, columns and series that filled his little red notebooks and their sports pages for the best part of the next four decades.

Successive generations of sports writers have told of how he taught them: "Fact is sacred, comment is free," how they should always ring back a new contact the following day and thank them for their help and that, when under pressure to fulfil the Saturday match report workload at Highbury or White Hart Lane that could read : 350 words Sunday Mirror/ 300 words Sunday Express/ 450 words News of The World/ 800 words (considered) Sunday Times/ 10 pars Sunday Telegraph – all ON THE WHISTLE - quotes to follow, they should follow the advice of one of his partners, Ron Roberts, and "breathe faster."

Reg rarely made a bad call when spotting young talent to develop but even when things didn't work out, he hated letting anyone go. The words "sack so-and-so" appeared at the top of the daily "to-do" list hammered out with two left-thumbs on the oldest noisiest typewriter in Fleet Street, every day, and one intended victim actually died in service of old age.

When he himself departed, two days after speaking at the Stanmore annual dinner, perhaps the most moving tribute appeared in the *Evening Standard*'s headline over a piece by another old boy, Michael Hart. Echoing the character made famous on the silver screen by Robert Donat, it read simply, "Goodbye Mr Hayter."

How he found the time to play cricket every summer, Saturday and Sunday, for Stanmore until he finally retired in his early 'seventies was beyond anyone but him.

The answer is that he had the constitution of a Pamplona bull and an almost spiritual commitment to mix business with pleasure. Most of all, he had the game he loved longer than anyone or anything else to remind him that good times were always just a perfect cover drive, a perfect leg cutter or a perfect glass of beer watching perfect sunset away.

CHAPTER 3

Other Events

One thing leads to another.

Christopher then attended an activity exhibition at The Birmingham Centre (1981) and came across a stand that was displaying "Hot Minis" – a plastic pouch, which when shaken caused the powder inside to give out heat. Following discussion with the stand holder, this led to becoming an agent and first, to find a sponsor and then, to do all the publicity for The Fosters British Water Ski Championships in 1983 when they were held at Bomere, near Shrewsbury. The stall holder's son was a water skier. The Federation arranged the accommodation, entries and competition, whilst the publicity officer gained the finance, publicity, arranged interviews with radio and television and wrote for the various media who would give the event coverage. It was early days for the sport, so it was necessary to build the excitement into the reports not just record what was happening. Although no world records were broken four world champions participated and a great atmosphere was established.

The overall winners were John Battleday and Dr Phillipa Masters, who won the ladies event.

Later in researching the values of the 'Hot Mini' (1983) he learnt that there was a Joint Services expedition planning to go to Brabant Island in the Antarctic for three years under canvas. He was to provide the publicity, gain finance and support with food, tents and materials for the explorers, who were led by Chris Furze, who had previously explored the same region. Each participant would go out for one or two years, nobody previously had attempted to stay solely under canvas in such sub zero and uncharted frozen wastes ever before. Their story in the book 'Elephant Island' is a wonderful read of endeavour, courage and fortitude. One deal that was arranged was that B.A.T. would supply cigarettes to the teams for the three years, our man's deal was ten per cent of all deals arranged, but chagrin, all cigarettes would go into bond and not be available in the UK before dispatch!!

On the playing front, Christopher had played against New Zealand and a few matches against Hampshire, besides many club games against varied opposition, his changed style to the bowling of slow medium variable paced outswing had proved extremely successful. It was to be challenged at top level – amongst strangers. The day in question dawned – rain for the first two hours, a guest of India Gymkhana at Uxbridge, the only white man on the field. The opposition: the full Indian Test squad, with the exception Mohinder 'Jimmy' Amarnath who changed sides. Our man did not have to wait long, he was brought on first change, Gaekwad the opening bat was facing and the fifth ball was chipped to extra cover who dropped it, but then a wicket fell at the other end, Kirti Azad came in, he batted five for India, full of confidence Kirti arranged to have a free hit with the wicket keeper, discussed in Hindi, (later it came to light he thought he could hit our man into the nearest flats) so down the pitch he came, missed the ball and was not stumped by agreement, luckily no further chances and he was caught next ball at Long off. Ravi Sastri entered and hit him for a six off his first ball, but off the third ball he was stumped, two wickets and two chances. But now it was serious, for the new batsman was Sunil Gavaskar (then the highest scoring batsman in Test Cricket), the first ball he pretended to come down the pitch and so our bowler dropped it shorter and Sunil cracked him past cover for four. However, no more short balls, he had the privilege of bowling fourteen balls to him and that was the only boundary, after six overs it was someone else's turn, our man had taken 2 for 36. But he would never be nervous bowling to anyone again.

The nineteen eighties saw him change course, still strongly in cricket, with *The Cricketer* now going from strength to strength, he had been given the opportunity to write feature articles, one of which developed into being a World Assessment of cricket equipment, clothing and footwear, which at its peak was around thirty thousand words. Companies who featured, found it a valuable sales medium, thus it made up to nearly £50 thousand in advertisement revenue.

One of the new products were Symonds cricket bats, which were based in Allahabad in India, a former frontier town, this company was run by two brothers, the eldest was Dips Banergee. They invited our man to visit them and would pay all his expenses in India if he could arrange his flight. Another friend Vikram Kaul, was acting Manager of Air India in London

Vikram came forward with a special fare and so he was India bound. Previously *The Cricketer* had taken a tour to Dubai, which had been reciprocated with tours to UK and Australia through our chap's contacts. Now the kindness was returned, he flew to Delhi, meeting up with the doyen supplier of cricket willow, the one and only Carlton Wright, who at the time was visiting the same factory, accompanied by his lovely niece, Helen Malcolm, the three first travelled to Aggra, arriving in the evening, this was special as they were able to visit the Taj Mahal in the dark. Not everyone realises that the marble is translucent, they all stayed till the following day to see its beauty in the sunshine, together with the wonderful views from all its four sides. The Banerjees were perfect hosts, taking the trio to The Red Fort, Fatepur Sikri, a fantastic swamp water birds sanctuary that in the days of The Raj, shooting parties would shoot thousands of game. Then back to Delhi and by train to Allahabad.

Next day was again special as Carlton celebrated his 70th birthday, this included a visit to the 'factory', where they had a platoon of soldiers – who formed a guard of honour for the birthday boy.

During that Winter England were touring India and the next day the Test Match started in Kanpur, to the trio's surprise they were staying in the same hotel as the players. What was to greet them they could never have expected, for the hotel was in a cul-de-sac and on the entrance to the road where armed soldiers, in the foyer and on each floor of the hotel. All rooms were searched for bombs, had they realised the full gravity of the situation they might have had nightmares, but it seemed the norm. The city was crammed with millions of people and although they had an Indian driver going to the ground was even more scarier. They found their seats in a special stand – all the ground was caged with high-wired sections, to move from one section to another meant searching out the guard commander, who in turn, would open a small gate at gunpoint.

As a white man you would find yourself circled ten deep by people who apparently had not seen white people previously. One night in the hotel they all met two of the Indian stars previously befriended – Ravi Sastri and Sunil Gavaskar. No time to relax, back in the car and off to Kanha National Park to search for tigers. On arrival at their jungle domain – it was were the Queen had stayed – it was situated on the side of a large river, Mr Banerjee said we should drive into the jungle 'to have a look' before the real hunting the next morning, whether it was the driver or bad luck we ended up stuck in the mud. No thought of the wild animals, WE are English, so we all pile out of the car and push and push several times and we survived. Maybe it was past the animals dinner time!! Early next morning we were out on elephants and although no tigers, we did visit Kiplings' Camp, set up by Rudyard Kipling. Real adventure, many animals, no tigers but wild bears, boar, and some snakes. Then by train to Bombay and indescribable Indian way of life, culture, smells, trains and stories.

Millions of people squeezed together, heat, beggars, thieves, a telephone system like non other and traffic – What an experience.

India is so different to everything western, to land at midnight at Delhi airport, muddle through customs and find a taxi driving along wide vistas with huge white marble buildings to a fabulous hotel, oblivious to the squalor and misery so close by. The eight hour flight had accustomed one to the people and everyone warned that eating and drinking was a hazard unless one concentrated and realised the necessity only to drink fluids that could not be contaminated, viz. alcohol, tinned juice or sealed fizzy drinks.

Never use ice, never eat salad, but curries were good because they would have been cooked for a long time. Bananas and oranges were safe because you peeled them yourself, great care was necessary at all times. Care had to be taken when moving into new sleeping arrangements or putting on footwear unless you took proper precautions. One never gave to beggars, and as crowds were the norm one looks after valuables conscientiously.

Obtain an Indian driver and hang on desperately, do not travel outside a city after 6 pm, unless in an armed convoy!!! Whether travelling by train or car be prepared to see all manner of ablutions and rituals as you pass by, try not to be shocked. Against such a backdrop there was majesty and mystique, long lost religious temples, days of the Raj, splendour of the Maharajahs and humour and children's naiveté. Driving down a road we came to a river that appeared more like a lake, so our driver walked ahead of the car to allow us to follow safely. Catching a train was also very different, often the train would have arrived before you reached the station and people lived on the platforms, the train would be twenty minutes in the station or even longer.

Passengers travel inside the long distance trains, but both inside and on top and on the sides of the local trains. One thing that should be central in your thinking, their culture tells them all that whatever agreement you make they will endeavour to improve on the arrangements or price and they are very good at dealing. There is a huge void between the 'Haves' and the 'Have Nots'.

It was at this time he was contacted by a Welsh company, who were thinking of starting a new Rugby journal, led by 'King' Barry John* and they consulted with him on its potential viability, the editorial staffing would be very strong. However, its success would be based on its potential advertisement revenue and how quickly it could generate circulation. Sadly the advice was not to publish, as the company did not have other titles or enough finance to guarantee the production costs for at least four issues.

The Cricketer's success now gave the company the opportunity to diversify and Ben Brocklehurst set up a tour company with holidays to Corfu, initially taking cricket teams to play against the three main clubs, they played on a matting pitch on sand and grass in the centre of the town of Corfu. The Greeks had their own rules. The boundary was where the cars were parked, when they batted they moved the cars close as possible and then when the opposition were batting the cars were moved further away. Often matches had delayed starts due to not finding stumps that had mysteriously vanished since the previous game. Ben always took one or two of his personal friends who would have been stars of yesteryear. His staff were also able to have a 'reduced priced' holiday, the great that accompanied our man was the former fighter ace and England cricketer Bill Edrich, one of the famous 'twins', to live and meet everyday your hero and even bat with him, could life be any better? Bill was a man, who believed every day was for living to the full. He would be the same, well almost, talking to any female, with the famous and with those who were not important. At three in the morning a few bevies would have passed his lips, but by nine am the next morning he was as fresh as a daisy, ready for whatever life would care to offer.

Today and Tomorrow was what he cared for, not his exploits and deeds past and he continued that philosophy right up to the end.

His 'twin' – Denis Compton – 'Compo' had the same knee problems as our man, therefore it was not surprising that they were introduced, Compo also worked in the advertising world, although not physically similar, the twins both worked hard at enjoying themselves. Sadly, like his twin he seldom recounted his achievements. Although he was a fantastic batsman with a marvellous flair for playing in an un-orthodox manner, there were as many stories about him losing pieces of equipment or his cricket bag than most. Other stories abounded about who and how he had run his partners out. But the strength of the character of the man was the respect, in which everyone held him. Years later at a Dinner, where he made his last public appearance – when he walked into the Banqueting Hall everybody rose to their feet and cheered, a reputation well earned.

When he died, the nation mourned. His Memorial service was held at Westminster Abbey, applications had to be submitted for the three thousand tickets, six thousand applied. Being on the Executive Committee of the Forty Club meant our man was there.

Supporting the success of the magazine, it ran national competitions, one of which was 'The National Village Cricket Knockout', with the final being played at Lord's, villages from England, Scotland and Wales competed in groups, the event had coverage in local papers, on radio and television. In the early years, our man ran a 'Throwing the cricket ball' competition. *The Cricketer* naturally had a box and Ben invited various personalities and staff to enjoy the occasion. One regular visitor was Sir Len Hutton, his son Richard married Ben's daughter Charmagne. Sir Len was the first professional to Captain England. He was a quiet gentle man with a dry humour and a man many had idolised, unlike many whom one meets, he was very worthy of the mantle which rested on his shoulders.

The next move was a direction change that to helping professional cricketers with their benefits, we have already mentioned Barry Richards and David Turner, others included Bob Stephenson, Tim Tremlett, Gordon Greenidge and Malcolm Marshall, Mark Nicholas and in 1995 Hampshire County Cricket Club.

The Gordon Greenidge benefit was particularly important for our man, for he helped to run the match against the Hampshire Hogs, Gordon was one of the finest opening batsmen of all time, with his partner Desmond Haynes representing West Indies. In the match our man bowled fifteen overs and took the first five batsmen's wickets for a personal tally of 71, Gordon the next man in took three runs from two overs, before he was taken off. Later when asked why he hadn't hit him out of the ground, he replied, "He had dispatched five of my mates, I was not going to be the sixth."

Everyone knew that had he wanted to, that is what would

have occurred, but it was his way of saying thank you to the organiser of his benefit match. Following the Match, our man managed Gordon for the next three years. Gordon was a family man and a private person and a very different personality when playing cricket. Initially when he was going abroad with the West Indian team our man would arrange activities for him to attend after the Test matches, but soon learnt that Mr Greenidge was only interested in playing at the highest level, invariably after the final Test Match Gordon would gain a previous injury which would necessitate his early return home.

One night watching late television, a programme appeared about a man called Tim Hudson, who had unusual views on sponsorship, man managership and marketing, a telephone call to the station next morning elicited how to make contact. His background had been as follows:

He was born the son of a cotton family in Lancashire, whilst learning the trade, he had also played 2nd XI cricket for the county. He was sent to London to further his training, one night he went to a party, at which there was a film star who said he looked like a disc jockey and that he should have a go for radio. Tim took the advice and went to Hollywood and became involved with rock music, the Beatles and 'flower power', he hosted a programme on Sunset Strip as well as making some deals on real estate.

But the ties with England and cricket were still magnetic, so he returned to Cheshire and bought Birtles Hall and created a cricket ground, to which he brought many cricketers of international status. He became Ian Botham's Manager, creating some single wicket matches. He had a flair for marketing and he created huge publicity, repeatedly gaining both television coverage and centre page spreads in the tabloids. Following discussion our man was asked to join him and this resulted in learning the marketing package. It was necessary to explain to Tim that some of his ideas were over the top, but it was also a large learning curve. Tim was generous both with introductions and the provision of a northern base of his house and telephone and all meals. This was in return for match planning and organisation combined with being a link-man. Ian Botham, Viv Richards and Brian Close were all regular visitors, talking into the night about the game they all loved. Brian was a very interesting man, who chain smoked, which was a strange factor when you considered he had played cricket to the highest level and played golf left and right handed to single figures. Rubbing shoulders with these greats gave one an opportunity very few were privileged so to do, life in those days was certainly never dull. At one time it was suggested that Ian Botham would star in a film, nobody believed it would happen, however, the link-man took the telephone call from the producer in Australia. This chapter of events lasted a year or two, then drugs became an issue and some bad publicity effected both Tim and Ian and the whole arrangement fizzled out, Tim and his wife Maxi returning to the States permanently – they had been going back most winters and that was the end of another saga.

Early in 1985 he was contacted by an Australian who was making coaching videos with Frank Tyson and had negotiated that the Prudential Assurance company was to sponsor the making and distribution of the product. So they looked for someone in the UK to organise and run the company. Meetings were arranged all over the Country and John Emburey accompanied him, meeting clubs and promoting the video sales. The video gave detailed instruction on bowling, batting and fielding, as well as wicket-keeping. A company had been set-up and things were progressing well, till suddenly the Australian organiser removed all the monies from the business.

Commander Christopher Furze
(Antarctic Explorer)

By Christopher Bazalgette

Following a difficult birth, Christopher was born with the cord around his neck. For the first eighteen months he was looked after by a nanny, as his parents were abroad in Hong Kong.

On the outbreak of the 2nd World War they returned to England, whereupon his father was made Naval Attache to Europe and was abroad for most of the war. Their farm in Kent was filled with evacuees and his Mother took him to the West Country, working on farms, they moved house frequently.

When aged four his Mother attempted to put him into school, but he refused and she ended up teaching him herself. Christopher was obsessed with birds, they used to go for walks by the river and on their return he would remember all the birds they had seen. All he talked about was birds, his Mother even had to read him four volumes of Thorburn's Book of birds. His parents pursued their own passion for painting – his Father for flowers and his Mother for landscapes, houses, trees and animals.

When aged six he wrote his first book, this was about birds, but this time about the ones he would see when he visited USA, Father had been transferred from Europe to America. The same year his Mother taught him to make lino-cuts and he made his own Christmas cards.

In 1948, now aged 13 he won a scholarship to Malvern College. His central interest was still natural history, although he had now progressed from drawings to paintings. He was tutored, with five other boys, by H.C.Wilson, of whom he speaks very highly, stating how Mr Wilson was brilliant if unconventional and 'over the top', this tutor also taught him to draw fast. Chemistry and Physics were also in the Syllabus. He contemplated studying medicine – his hero was Eric Ennion who was a GP and painted birds for pleasure.

In 1951 his parents moved to Scotland, twenty miles from the Grampians, and they set up a ski club. So on arriving for the Christmas holidays he was soon kitted out for skiing, he took to it like a 'duck to water'. One of his Father's friends ran a similar Climbing Club, by the New Year his fate was sealed. His last two years at Malvern were split between sport and Biology and drawing seriously.

His Father sponsored him for two weeks on Fair Isle in October where Ken Williamson was warden of the Bird Sanctuary, when his theory on Drift Migration was very new. Christopher learnt how to ring birds and was privileged to see Ken catching a corncrake by hand.

Having left school, it was natural to follow his Father into the Royal Navy, he spent three months at Dartmouth, followed by HMS Triumph- the cadet training ship. His adventure had begun; - first they rescued SS Empire Windrush, which caught fire whilst bringing troops home from Korea, helping to douse the flames and taking the injured to Tunis. This was followed by clearing-up after an earthquake in Greece. Prior to going to the Royal Naval Engineering College at Plymouth he worked in HMS Jamaica and Corunna. He played for the RNEC rugby team in 1956/7 and they won all their matches. One Spring he camped on the Isle of Coll drawing and bird watching, also at RNEC he crewed in several cross channel Ocean races.

At this time the Navy were promoting Outward Bound activities, Christopher was lucky, for his Divisional Officer fixed a 2-week course in the Cairngorms and he was the only student of 22 who knew the range. He became unofficial adviser on which route to take and the gear they would require. They went in October when it was cold and snowy, although everyone else were inexperienced, nobody was injured. Three, including Christopher went over the top and down the steep NE slope, they only just found the Shelter Stone in heavily drifted snow. At Easter 1957 he and two others skied at Mjolfjell in Norway and he returned for two more summers.

The following year Commander Malcolm Burley (Dartmouth) organised and led an expedition to Hardangervidda in Norway and agreed Christopher could join them.

Two years passed at RNC Greenwich – During which time he married and returned to his drawing and painting.

Then in 1969, he heard Malcolm Burley was leading a Joint Services Expedition to Elephant Island, the first, since the island was made famous by Ernest Shackleton in 1916. The interview was stringent but his earlier experience enabled him to pass and he was given the tasks of surveying the island's birds and cox'n of the Gemini dinghy. The build-up included a two-week mountaineering course in Glenmore, with professionals like John Cunningham and Chouinard. This first trip went perfectly and was a new beginning for Lieutenant Commander Christopher Furse.

Two years were spent on *Ark Royal* hanging onto his dream to return to the Arctic, his last month before handing over to his replacement enabled him to complete his ornithological study from Elephant Isle for the 1970/71 survey. This report was now delivered to the British Antarctic Survey (BAS) to show them he was worth their support in any follow-up expedition. After *Ark Royal* he was promoted to Commander and sent to a shore posting, Three years to plan and organise.

On this first trip to Elephant, the leader and Christopher were setting up a dump in calm weather when they were suddenly called by radio to get to the 'chopper' landing site, because bad weather was in the offing. They were flown back to the ship, hove-to in a Force 10 wind, which continued for two days. Had we missed the flight we would have had to paddle four hundred miles to the South Orkneys or 800 to South Georgia. I had scared myself stiff driving our only Gemini dinghy with one small outboard for 5 weeks round 10km of floating snout of Endurance Glacier.

For his expedition Chris decided it would be safer to use canoes round the coasts. But they would need modifying, which we did to ten Tasmans we bought. In the Spring we advertised for applicants from all the Services.

Then we received a rumour HMS *Endurance* might be scrapped (without her we could not reach our destination), we continued to plan – hoping –.

Then Chris received a message from a friend on the Naval staff – it read:

'Endurance is running on to 1977'

There had been an 'incident' in 1976, when an Argentinean warship fired a shot across the bows of RRS *Shackleton* off the Falkland Islands. A few years later someone told him there had been an escalation of hostility by the Argentineans, this changed the Government's mind, Endurance was saved and they had a fantastic expedition.

In 1980 he started to organise a more complicated expedition to Brabant Island (1983 –1985) this would be in three phases further down the Antarctic peninsular. The party would again depend on HMS *Endurance* to transport each phase. As in 1976, in June 1981 *Endurance* was given notice of being scrapped in 1982. Christopher pretended to arrange other ways to transport the party to and from Brabant – friends in MOD/Navy provided rations and fuel and he paid for its transportation to Port Stanley in time for Captain

Barker in Endurance to pick up in March 1982. He landed then at USARP Palmer Station on Anvers island during Endurance's last deployment. The ship was due to return to Britain on April 1st. On 2nd April Argentina invaded the Falklands – it finally returned in August, and the scrapping was removed.

Captain Barker's book 'Beyond Endurance' tells a lot of truths before and after.

Hence Endurance carried out all our changeovers, for this expedition would be totally under canvas. Our three phases were:

1st Summer party ten men from late December 1983 to mid March 1984, winter party - twelve men from mid March 1984 to mid December 1984 and 2nd Summer party from mid December 1984 to mid March 1985.

In November 1983 Christopher Furse needed professional help to raise funds for his forthcoming expedition, through his photographer Jed Corbett he met Chris Bazalgette and consequently he became involved with this venture. His role was to create funding from companies interested in sponsorship of British enterprise; support in supplying tents,

Specially designed anoraks and equipment and stores from breakfast serials to cigarettes. When that role finished my activity was to organise and operate the Press links and departure conferences.

Brabant Island was thoroughly explored and most of it was climbed. The major achievement was to demonstrate that relying on tents and snowholes in winter was safe in winter in that region. Their success will make it easier for small economical expeditions to gain approval.

After this expedition, Christopher Furze was contacted by Peter Steer, the Executive Director of the British Schools Exploring Society (BSES) in 1985 to speak at their Dinner, he had been a Fellow of the Royal Geographical Society since

1971, but had never heard of BSES. The youngsters had proved themselves in Iceland and Lapland, so I told them now they should look further afield, and how lucky they were. He must have struck the right note as then he was asked to lead a 6-week expedition for BSES to Spitzbergen in Summer 1987, the organisation would fund a recce for HIM and another, in 1986, which, with his contacts went well.

John Battleday

By Christopher Bazalgette

John Battleday was born in Melbourne, Australia, of English parents in 1957. The family later moved to Malta. When he was eight years old they bought a motor-boat and his father introduced his son to waterskiing.

With the sea so close he learnt quickly and by the time the family had returned to the United Kingdom he was able to compete in the under 16 junior competition aged just twelve.

A year later he had been picked for the English Junior team, following this up two years later by being selected for the Senior team – now only sixteen.

Dedication and determination were two very prominent parts of John's character, for it appeared John's life had been planned to follow his sporting prowess. Within two years in 1975 he was third in the European Championships and eighteenth in the world, competing in Bogota, Columbia. Training was paramount and every year his improvement was noticeable.

In 1976 competing in the British Championships he was second overall, second in ski jumping and only third in Tricks as this was his strongest discipline.

Like everything else in life, nothing is ever straight forward. He was now hit with a period of injuries and it took him to 1981 when the World Championships were held at Thorpe Park, for him to be competitive at the highest level. He came second overall, which considering the standard of waterskiing around the world, this was a huge achievement.

In 1983 (when Christopher Bazalgette helped run the Championships at Bomere Lake, Nr Shrewsbury, finding Fosters Lager as sponsors and doing all the press coverage) four World Champions participated but John Battleday won. In the same year he was third in the world.

His other successes included four European Slalom championships and also winning the European water ski Tricks event.

In Tricks, when he first became the British champion his total points were 5660, over the next twenty years he steadily built up the annual points tally till when he retired from competition he had put the record up to 8650 points, the mark of a true champion.

Having made his mark in the sport the natural progression was to start his own ski school. From his early twenties he had been coaching and on retirement from competition decided this would be his future role.

He now has three boat lakes and a cable ski facility. He can boast it is the premier boat and cable tournament site in the United Kingdom based at Thorpe Park.

They offer everything including a kids club in the summer (note under '16's need parental supervision) ski and wakeboard instruction, slalom, tricks and jumping, instructor and driver courses for boats, together with a fully stocked shop.

John is very approachable and since his early days has been a great ambassador for the sport.

Sir Len Hutton
b. June 1906 – d. September 1990

By Keith Moss MBE

Leonard was the youngest of five children of Henry and Lily Hutton in Fulneck. In 1992 a blue plaque was unveiled at No 5 to commemorate the birth.

Len Hutton was brought up within the strict structure of the Moravian movement in Fulneck, a mile from the centre of Pudsey. Pudsey, the buffer state between Leeds and Bradford famed as the place where the 'birds fly backurds to keep the muck out of their eyes, for its renowned treacle mines'. Today the birds fly straighter, due to the withdrawal of the EU subsidy with the result the treacle mines have gone into liquidation.

This was and still is today a settlement of the Moravian Church. Moravians were the earliest Protestant sect in the 15th Century, with their beginnings in Bohemia. They arrived in England in the 1730's and put down roots in Fulneck in 1745. Becoming a self contained community that established a tradition of Christian disciplines, hard work, self-sufficiency and a simple and unworldly faith. John Wesley visited them in 1780 and noted in his diary that there were a hundred young men, fifty young women, many widows and a hundred married persons all employed from morning to night for no wages save a little plain food and raiment.

Like serving on the old Yorkshire committee!

Their tradition expressed in doing what you had to do thoroughly and to the best of your ability: this was a precept Len adhered to throughout his life.

The Moravian church has a strong presence in the West Indies, both Curtly Ambrose and Sir Vivian Richards are both Moravians.

Benjamin Hutton, Len's great, great grandfather was born in Perth (Scotland) in 1763 and moved to Yorkshire soon afterwards.

So the young Hutton grew up in a structured happy environment playing cricket with his brothers in the fields behind his home or on the road, due to the little traffic, with cricket balls made in the mills out of cloth cut-offs. It was a case of Chapel twice a day on Sunday, Boys Brigade, the institute and watching Gilbert and Sullivan performances by the Operatic Society, in which his three maiden aunts were leading members.

The Minister from 1928-1932 was Rev Charles Millowes, the archetypal cricketing parson, who played for Fulneck and Pudsey St Lawrence midweek team and a great supporter of Len. Even when young Len was too good for Fulneck, so it was natural for him to follow his elder brothers to Pudsey St Lawrence.

He made his debut in the Bradford League aged 13. This was one of the most competitive leagues in the county. It is beyond doubt that this league experience was to serve him well in his future career. Two people were pivotal in his development, the first was Herbert Sutcliffe who lived a quarter mile away and was instrumental with Richard Ingham, a former President of Pudsey St Lawrence and on the Yorkshire committee, in getting Len to attend Easter nets in 1930. This culminated in their great Yorkshire opening partnership of Hutton and Sutcliffe.

Another supporter was Edgar Oldroyd, a typical Yorkshire pro of the period, he left the County in 1931 and became pro at Pudsey St Lawrence the following year.

Len, aged 16 was his opening partner. He learnt much from the older man; the art of playing spin, batting on a sticky wicket and very importantly the art of defence. He also learnt about the culture of playing for the county club, a side he was to grace from 1934 to 1955. One priceless benefit was to give him a tangible link with Hirst and Rhodes, the very bedrock of Yorkshire cricket. His education was further enhanced on his first tour, this to Jamaica in 1936. Not yet 20 he learnt much about his colleagues in that great pre war team. The next four years he consolidated his spot as Yorkshire's opening batsman and after 0 and 1 against New Zealand in 1937 as England's No.1, except for a selectorial blip in 1948, until his retirement from Test cricket in 1955. Two other factors helped his development, on the field Ticker Mitchell would, from the other end, chide him for thinking about a run 'Keep defending' was the cry. Off the field young Len would talk long into the evening with two great students and practitioners of the game – Bill Bowes and Hedley Verity.

The final two years of the decade were indeed halcyon days. August 1938 will be forever etched in the history of cricket, he scored 364 against Australia at the Oval in the mammoth time of 13 hours and twenty minutes, a truly great performance, a triumph of skill, perseverance and not least stamina. England rejoiced, none more so than in Pudsey, where the church bells were pealed 364 times.

Later that year he toured South Africa with MCC finishing with an average of 64.88.

1939 was an even better season, scoring 2883 runs at 62.67 and for good measure he took 44 wickets bowling leg spin and googlies at an average of 18.68, third in the county averages to Verity and Bowes, plus taking 38 catches. He had 52 innings and bowled 220 eight ball overs. Todays' players say they play too much cricket!

Then tragedy struck in March 1941, when he fractured his left forearm whilst attempting a 'fly-spring' in the gymnasium on an army PTI course. After numerous operations he left the Army with his left arm two inches shorter than his right. In that he was able to resume Test cricket after the war speaks volumes for his determination and tenacity.

I first saw Len as a player in 1943 when he again played for Pudsey St Lawrence, every side had a number of Test and county cricketers. But like life all was not plain sailing for Len.

He lost the captaincy of Pudsey and they would not release him to play for England, instead he played against Lidget Green, Pelham Warner was not happy. It is true to say Len did not enjoy the happiest relationships with the club committee, who found it against their nature to pay him £100 per season.

Graciously Len's response was to place on record that in the 70's and 80's he was always made very welcome, he also stated that many of his most blissful hours of his life were at Pudsey St Lawrence.

In the post war years his achievements tell the story of this remarkable cricketer. Both as a player and captain he held England's batting together repeatedly bearing the brunt of the attack against Lindwall and Miller, especially being successful in 1946/47 and 1948. Much as 1939 had been good for him so was 1949. He had 56 innings made 3429 runs including 12 centuries and took 41 catches but only seven wickets bowling.

His appointment as England Captain in 1952 was well deserved, as was the famous victory at the Oval that won the Ashes. Times were different then comparing that victory to the one in 2005. First we saw Len waving to a huge crowd below him and then retiring to cut the celebration cake with the Australian skipper – Lindsay Hassett and the Australian team in the players' dining room, all players immaculate in suit or blazer. One other illustration of change – on the day before the final Test Len was playing for Yorkshire against Derbyshire at Scarborough, the match finishing at 3.15 pm, then a tough drive to London (no motorways), and no days off before a Test Match in those days.

I believe his absolute moment of glory was when he retained the Ashes in 1954/55 largely through his astute captaincy and the superb performances of Statham and Tyson, backed by Bob Appleyard and Trevor Bailey. I had nothing but the greatest admiration for the way he tackled his appointment as England's Captain, the Establishment were not totally in favour – a professional and a Yorkshireman to boot did not go down too well.

How well deserved the knighthood bestowed on him by the Queen in 1956.

1988 was a memorable year the 50th anniversary of his 364 runs, a wonderful dinner at the Queens Hotel Leeds. Memorable speeches by Brian Walsh, Dennis Compton, Fred Trueman and to end the evening superb reply by the Guest of Honour. Not a bad top table: Cyril Washbrook, Tom Graveney, Bob Appleyard, Ray Lindwall, Peter May, Colin Cowdrey, Godfrey Evans and Neil Harvey.

August 1990. Len and Dorothy spent the week with Jean and myself at Eastbourne to watch the county play Sussex. I was deeply concerned about his health. He seemed to be failing, but he still took his Yorkshire Presidential duties very seriously. The match coincided with the funeral in Eastbourne of Ian Gow, the towns' M.P. who had been murdered by terrorists. At the time of the Funeral both teams lined up for a minutes silence in respect. Len insisted in lining up with the teams. As we know he passed away in the September.

How do you sum up such a brilliant career?

Batsmanship beyond compare, Perfect balance at the crease, Slight movement back before the shot is played. His defensive qualities, honed to perfection with the Mitchells and the Oldroyds, were a joy to see.

To see him bat on a Park Avenue 'sticky' was a joy to behold, the peerless craftsman in complete control. We remember him most however for that most sumptuous of strokes, the cover drive, made in heaven, Headingley and Lords. He cut the hook shot out after his injury. He did not need it. He most certainly was not flamboyant, he was the consummate stylist.

Colin Shakespeare captured the very essence of Len's batsmanship in his splendid poem:

To Sir Len Hutton

There was no violence in him, rather
The quiet mathematician
Given over to geomatrics
And the study of angles,
Arcs,
Perimeters and Perpendiculars
Curves and dividing lines,
But rarely, rarely
The parabola.

And the mystery of it all
Was the mastery of it all.

Comment by Keith Moss
Having known Len very well I would like to add my own feelings, he was a vulnerable man, of economy of timing, enigmatic in his conversation. Often he seemed to speak in riddles, then saying 'see what I mean'. Above all he bore the trappings of true greatness with a quiet calm dignity, humility and determination. His Moravian background and upbringing served him well.

Barry John

By Robert Kitson

Even now they still call him by his Christian name. Or just 'The King'. For those growing up in Wales in the late 1960s and 1970s, Barry John was as famous as Elvis Presley, if not more so. Imagine the combined public profiles of Johnny Wilkinson and David Beckham squeezed into the parochial goldfish bowl of Welsh rugby. The greatest fly-half the British Isles has ever produced often felt under less pressure on the field of play.

These days, with agents and sponsorship endorsements and electronic gates, it might all have turned out differently. Back then, though, there was no escape. At the age of just 27, at the peak of his career, having just steered Wales to a grand slam, rugby's answer to George Best could take no more. The finality, they say, was when he visited a hospital in Swansea and a young girl curtsied to him on arrival. The same thing happened shortly afterwards in Rhyl. The unassuming lad who grew up in a Welsh mining village, Cefneithin, simply wanted to be treated like anyone else.

Reading the relevant passages of his autobiography now is to be reminded of a world before the X-Factor or Britain's Got Talent, when fame was thrust upon individuals who never craved it. "At first it was all fun," wrote John rather wistfully in 1974. "But in the last year of my career, and particularly when I got back from the 1971 Lions tour of New Zealand, the pressures became more than I could stand. The former simplicity of my life was suddenly altered. Eventually I grew to loathe talking about rugby. I began to scream inwardly. It began to worry me that adulation was alienating me from the human race."

When he ate out in restaurants, he started to hear fragments ofother people's conversations. 'He's not very big, is he?'... 'I thought his hair was darker than that.' It merely increased the thunderous roar of the demons within his own head. "Occasionally I had the curious sensation of not being in my own body, of looking at it as if I were some kind of robot." When people say international sportsmen have it easy, they forget the amateur era when players were lucky to be allowed a little time off from work to represent their country.

That said, the professional game might not have suited Barry John, either. Endless training sessions and restrictive game plans would have straitjacketed his genius even more.

For the beauty of Barry lay in his instinctive grasp of the game of rugby union. The official history of the Welsh Rugby Union described it thus: "The clue to an understanding of his achieved style lies in what he could make others do to themselves. The kicking, whether spinning trajectories that rolled away or precise chips or scudding grubbers, was a long-range control, but his running - deft, poised, a fragile illusion that one wrong instant could crack, yet rarely did - was the art of the fly-half at its most testing. He was the dragonfly on the anvil of destruction. John ran in another dimension of time and space. His opponents ran into the glass walls which covered his escape routes from their bewildered clutches. He left mouths, and back rows, agape."

He was, in other words, an oval ball magician. As his fame grew, he found opponents would stand off him a little, conscious they were about to be wrong-footed. It merely gave their tormentor more time to do so. Having caught the eye for Llanelli, he was first capped for Wales at the age of 21 whilst a student in Carmarthen and represented his country on 25 occasions. His global reputation was truly forged, however, in a different red jersey, that of the British and Irish Lions. Having been forced to return home early from the 1968 Lions tour of South Africa with a broken collarbone, he was initially in two minds as to whether to accept the invitation to go to New Zealand in 1971. Eventually the presence of the inspirational Welsh Coach, Carwyn James, who also hailed from Cefneithin, persuaded him it could be an experience worth sharing. It was to prove that and more. New Zealanders still rate the 1971 Lions as the best team ever to visit their shores. John was the kingpin, torturing the All Black full-back Fergie McCormick in the first Test with his tactical kicking. Despite losing the second Test, the Lions won the third and drew the fourth to win the series. John scored 30 of the Lions' 48 points over the four Tests, proving to the Kiwis that flair, guile and unorthodox thinking could outwit even the most organised of opponents.

By March 1972, the spell was broken. John's final game was against France in Cardiff, by which time he had already made up his mind to quit. In his last three international games he scored 35 points and became the highest points scorer in Welsh rugby history.

And then, as if a free-flowing tap had been turned off, he was gone. Maybe it was just as well people did not see him toiling, like Elvis, at the tail-end of his career. Ultimately, though, he felt unable to stay for the sake of his own sanity. The King chose to abdicate but his imperishable legacy lives on.

Sir Ian Botham OBE

By Christopher Bazalgette

This is about the man and my experience with him and his family, you can read of his many brilliant cricket achievements in a number of publications, not least *The Wisden Cricket Almanac* for the years he was playing for Somerset, Worcestershire or Durham or his International career for England in Test Matches and One Day Internationals.

Whilst I was watching television I came across an item about a man called Tim Hudson. He was mad about cricket and was about to manage Ian Botham.

The next day I telephoned the television station and found out how to make contact, this was successful and I became part of the team.

First I set up a press conference for Ian Botham, this was to be in Somerset and was successful. We then went to Cheshire – Birtles Hall – the home and headquarters of The Hudsons. Tim and Maxi Hudson had made money on the U.S.A. property market and involved with 'Flower Power' on Sunset Strip and various stars and now hoped to improve the marketing of cricket, with Ian Botham as their first star.

Tim set about developing a cricket ground - known as 'Birtles Bowl' within the grounds. The idea was to play special matches with international stars making up the teams.

Every day one met various cricketers of great repute, Beefy and Vivian Richards were regulars as were Brian Close and Franklyn Stephenson.

Ian Botham grew up and had great support from loving parents, showed promise from an early age and even repeatedly told his careers master that he was going to be a professional sportsman, when the teacher challenged him, he obtained permission not to attend the class as it was a waste of time.

Each step up the ladder was gained by proving his ability against older boys. He continued to be super confidant and the rest is history. Life however, does provide you with tests of character, nothing is plain sailing and you have to work for your success.

Ian overcame hurdle after hurdle and through his life has chosen cricket, football and now golf, honesty and fair play and to do your best and to play for England. Such standards have marked him apart.

Years later, I read in a newspaper that he had not trained properly and he lacked professional discipline whilst abroad on tour. I knew that was rubbish, as this man is and always has been a complete professional sportsman, who had pride in performance and would not jeopardise the quality of his play. For all the time I knew him he was scrupulous about his early morning training runs, totally dedicated to keeping fit – without any personal trainer.

Like any fit sportsman he would have a beer with the next man and also enjoyed his wine, it did not mean he would regularly be legless, in fact before a big innings or match he would act responsibly. In the two years I knew him well he was always a very pleasant and super chap to be around – Full of 'bon viveur' and fun – mischievous but never aggressive. I will never forget a moment of conversation I was having with Brian Close, standing near us was a boy of seven – Liam, Ian's son – he waited till our chat lessened – he needed to pass between us – and said 'Excuse me Sir, can I pass please?' Such excellent manners, were in my book the result of polite parents.

I was also present at a press lunch in Mayfair, when a press man called out to me that he had heard Beefy was 'smoking pot at Birtles' and could I confirm it? Not only did I refute the accusation strongly, as the Hudsons never allowed anybody to smoke inside Birtles Hall, other than Brian Close, I knew as I smoked cigarettes. I also challenged the man to withdraw his remarks or I would have to report him. I followed up with a report to Mr Hudson and Mr Botham and the matter was put in the hands of solicitors.

Sir Ian Botham was and is the most loyal of men, several years after the Birtles saga, I was visiting a cricket equipment exhibition in Bournemouth, Beefy, as he was then, had flown down to see one of his sponsors for a half an hour, whilst talking he noticed my wife standing about twenty yards way and insisted she should come over and be with us. From all the people he met every day he had remembered her from staying in the same house for a few days atleast four years earlier. Unlike many international stars this gentleman could always be relied upon and would recognise you for yourself not for whom you were from a status point of view,

On several occasions he was accused by the gutter press – not the cricket journalists – of assignations with young females whenever he was on tour, initially this was very upsetting to his family, until they realised the only way to counter the situation, was that he should have a member of his family as chaperone.

As there was always some freeloader who wanted to create a story.

One day when I was on my own at Birtles, the telephone rang and it was that Film Producer from Australia. I took the call that suggested Beefy was to become a film star, although the idea was not to be, I knew it was for real, not as the papers portrayed it as a 'Hudson whim' for the press.

Ever since boyhood Beefy believed, with total confidence, that he would be a successful sportsman. In the early days it might have been football or cricket, but when opportunity beckons… So cricket it was and his confidence won through.

Nothing in life is easy, there were many hurdles to overcome, many times a lesser man might have given up, but not Beefy and that is why he was so successful, convinced he was doing the right thing. When one day he had to go to hospital for treatment on a broken toe, he happened to enter a ward for children with Leukaemia, he was shocked to learn that some of them had only a short time to live, he vowed he would do all he could to improve their lot. This was the incentive he had to walk and raise huge funds. Now he has raised over ten million pounds. In 2003 he became the first President of Leukaemia Research. In 1992 He was given an OBE and then he was knighted in 2007.

Well done Sir Ian and Lady Kath.

CHAPTER 4

Centenary and Bicentenary

What happens when you reach forty?

As 1986 was the 99th year for the Hampshire Hogs, several plans were made to celebrate the Centenary, surprisingly with only six months to go and nobody had raised the thought of writing a history. Our man offered to have a go, never having written a book before. Surprisingly, he was availed on all sides on how to write it, who should be included and left out, and who would proof his copy. His wife went to local libraries, he interviewed the bold, gained others to write on tours and specific eras. He then put it all together, but then realised to publish it, it needed to be designed and his budget was just £2,000 for everything. The project should have taken 2-4 years, but he had six months from day one to delivery at the launch dinner. Sadly, the proof readers melted away when they were told they could not change it. Obviously it could have been better, but at least the club had a record of the first hundred years and the oldest members had imparted their memories before 'falling off the perch'. The book was duly delivered on the night, at the In and Out Club.

One early morning in February 1987, it was cold and cloudy, snow covering the ground, there were a few groups of people huddled together against the wind in a churchyard in West Meon in Hampshire. The day was when Sir Colin Cowdrey would lay the wreath on Sir Thomas Lord's grave, to mark the launch of the Bi-Centenary of the Marylebone Cricket Club. Our man was there and as the Rector was discussing with Sir Colin what would occur – in the church, those journalists and others who had journeyed from London had no idea where the grave was due to the blanket of snow. Our man knew and therefore in his own way started the proceedings by wiping away the snow in preparation of laying the wreath.

Then 'out of the blue' he received a telephone call from a reader of *The Cricketer*, who mentioned that cricket was being played in Europe. He followed this up and through a contact in Switzerland he was passed to another in Singapore, who had researched those countries who had started playing cricket.

This was 1989, in 1900 cricket had been played in the Olympic Games that were held in Paris, a team called the Devon Wanderers from England won the Gold medal, the Silver went to France and Belgium won the bronze. Through the Army of the Rhine, cricket was being played in Germany mainly by ex-pats. However, there were two leagues in Switzerland, Luxembourg had one team and cricket was an emerging game in both Austria and Italy. There was more cricket being played in Spain and Portugal, besides Malta and Gibraltar, started by those of the Royal Navy during the 2nd World War. One of the leading administrators was an Italian Simone Gambino. This 'gentleman' maintained the only way forward was to dictate that countries could only be represented if they included indigenous cricketers excluding all ex-patriots from other cricketing nations.

Not to be thwarted our man, in conjunction with *The Cricketer*, organised and ran 'The European Cricketer Cup' for ten nations in Guernsey in 1990, this was only possible through the great help and support of John Appleyard, a resident and former Captain of Hertfordshire and the current Captain of the Channel Islands cricket team. The Channel

Isles Tourist Board sponsored the event. The Countries who attended were Belgium, France, West Germany, Luxembourg, Spain, Greece, Malta, Austria, Switzerland and Guernsey. Many of the leading cricketing press visited Guernsey for the event and radio put out coverage before, during and after the competition.

Several of the teams included English, Indian and Pakistan players, some had to wait for visas and their route to Guernsey required special planning so as not to refuse entry. One team had to sleep on camp beds in a scout hut as funds were minimal, another team failed to pay their hotel account.

Guernsey beat France in the final.

But when the tournament wound up with a Gala Dinner at the King George V ground, everybody complimented the organisers on their initiative. Ben Brocklehurst Chairman of *The Cricketer* proposed a toast to Guernsey, 'Cricket' was toasted by His Excellency Lt.General Sir Alexander Boswell KCB CBE and Colin Cowdrey CBE, The Kent and England Captain (later Lord Cowdrey of Tonbridge) Replied. Two years later the event was repeated at Worksop College where Roger Knight (the former Surrey County cricketer, who later became MCC Secretary/Chief Executive), was Headmaster. On that occasion Germany were the victors, this time beating Belgium and the day following the Final they travelled to London to play MCC at Lord's Ground, this time followed by a Dinner at Lord's. Portugal had gained the required status and replaced Guernsey and Italy also had been allowed to enter. Christopher Martin-Jenkins and Sir Leon Brittain made speeches, both thanked our man for his initiative and organisation.

In the build-up for this event that was held on cricket grounds around Nottinghamshire, our usual leading television/radio man Christopher Martin-Jenkins was unavailable, so it was down to our man to do all the radio and television publicity for the event, invaluable experience for future activities.

Seventeen years later thirty-six European countries play cricket.

A worthy tribute to the research and efforts made by our man and *The Cricketer*'s sponsorship.

Back to 1990, on returning from Guernsey he received a telephone call from Peter Graves, the former prolific run scoring batsman for Sussex CCC, who was responsible for the British contingent at Golden Oldies Festivals, an event organised by Air New Zealand, held every two years, alternating in the northern or southern hemisphere, then being held the following month in Vancouver, British Columbia. He needed a journalist to write the newsletters for the event, it was a little ambiguous as whether there would be others to help him. Approximately two thousand cricketers and supporters would attend. Previous Festivals had taken place in New Zealand, England and Australia. The 'Form' was that teams of cricketers from all over the world, together with wives, girl friends and family would come on tour – the festival lasted for a week, three matches would be played, with a starting buffet evening party with cabaret and an end of party gala Dinner. He naturally accepted. He would be flown Air Canada – first class to Vancouver, all accommodation, internal travel and meals would be free in return for his writing a 'humorous' newsletter. As he was not attached to any specific team he was seconded to and welcomed by the Auckland Cricket Society, who had entered two teams, but were a man short, they gave him a huge welcome. But there was an even better surprise their unofficial manager was the former Test cricketer Bert Sutcliffe – a New Zealand superstar together with his beautiful wife Norma. The flight was idyllic, as the pilot flew between snow coated peaks, just out of reach on each wing tip and swooping down past Whistler mountain, still displaying weekend skiers on its upper slopes, Vancouver's winter playground.

The first match was played against an Australian side that included the Aussie Test leggie John Gleeson. During the event renewed contact was made with Richard Hadlee and a new contact was made with Jack Simmons, the Lancastrian county cricketer. Each team was allotted a group of 'Gophers', in the case of Auckland these were six gorgeous young ladies, who accompanied our team whenever a trip was made, for instance, on one of the occasions, the teams had lunch half way up Whistler mountain, the only route up or down was by cable car. When it was time to return our man had to meet the overall Director in the early evening, so descended with his team of Gophers, much to the chagrin of the other male team-mates.

The Director was Cliff Cox, formerly of the D'Oyly Carte Opera Company, and had several stage shows running in Vancouver. Our man was invited backstage and then off to Dinner. One exciting element that was seen daily was that flying boats would be landing and taking off to ferry people around the area, life was very relaxed and crime was minimal, often late into the night groups of all ages would be talking around the city. Most of the cricket was played on matting pitches and due to the number of teams matches were also played at the Victoria island. The Auckland cricket tour party all assembled in one room before the party returned to New Zealand, besides the convivial evening and the saying of goodbyes, there was an outstanding finale for our man – their whole group sang 'Now is the Hour' in Maori, a very moving send off.

The chance meeting with Jack Simmons resulted in his being able to make a rather important contract a few weeks after his return from Canada.

When he had managed Gordon Greenidge he had

negotiated the contract for the bat endorsement with a Sri Lankan, named, Harry Solomons (who ran the biggest cricket sales store in Australia and the world), as time passed they kept in contact with each other and became good friends. One day Harry telephoned him and asked if he could arrange a contract in the Lancashire League for the coming season for a young allrounder friend of Harry. So Jack Simmons was contacted and the matter was arranged – the young man was Steve Waugh, who became one of the World's best batsmen and Captain of Australia.

Prior to the Summer of 1992 arrangements were being put in hand for the 2nd European Cricketer Cup (previously reported), but due to the success of the reporting of the Golden Oldies event in Vancouver he was now invited to the next one in Canterbury, south island of New Zealand. He travelled with the English contingent under the guidance of Gullivers Sports Tours, flying first to Los Angeles for a two-day stopover, travelling with the team was John Appleyard, who since the European event had moved to Malta and another friend Dennis Carlstein, from South Africa. Besides going to Disney World, some practice was taken with an LA team. Then, the next stopover was on the beautiful island of Fiji, the hotel had a bar in the lagoon, with three restaurants and dancing every night, a long sandy beach and swaying palm trees, everybody you meet smiles and says 'Bola'. Possibly with the exception of those in your party, who should not have come down to breakfast. The Fijians are extremely friendly and anyone wanting an idyllic setting with romance, sand and relaxation should visit Fiji. Our guy had the fortune of 'rooming' with a great chap called 'Sumo' Clarke, who gave him a lovely memento in lace depicting the Golden Oldies. When travelling around the island one would see squads of youngsters practising rugby, which is their national sport. A game of cricket had been organised with some of their players, everyone took turns in scoring, our players were offered Fijian champagne – the only similarity with its French counterpart is that is an alcoholic drink – it is made from a root, the fluid looked like dishwater and one presumed tasted like it, not that dishwater is a favourite tipple. Not wishing to offend them several players did try it, luckily our man's fellow Fijian scorer offered to drink his remaining half pint, a lucky escape. Sadly next day was 'goodbye to Fiji, hello Auckland', but only a touchdown to meet the hosts – this is Headquarters for Air New Zealand, the organising body for Golden Oldies, then re- embark for the trip to Christchurch, on the South island. This is known as the Garden City and flowers with bright colours that delivered generous perfume. As Gullivers were the official Tour organisers our party had a very smart hotel in the City centre. The City is well laid out, with broad main roads, modern buildings and huge parks, plus a very old university, called 'Christ's College'.

Hardly had one had time to unpack when our man was summoned to the reception, one of his advertisers, who had been on holiday from Saratoga, had heard who were due in and had waited to meet him, before flying home. Laurence Parry, ran tours from Florida, another outpost where the game is important, although the meeting was very short, here was another illustration of how friendships are built through the noble game.

Auckland Cricket Society now had a paid-up member and therefore his three matches were guaranteed, during one of the games, batting at five he had a partnership of seventy plus, his partner was to remember this several years later. On the day when the teams were entertained at a special attraction they went to Akaroa, where the French landed and the place still carries many French street names. Several of the townsfolk turned out on a very wet day, to show everybody various methods of hand weaving – this being the land of the sheep.

Many international touring teams who visited Canterbury, always played a friendly match at a very small special ground called 'The Valley of Peace', a delightful haven, very similar to an English club ground. It was reached across a wooden bridge. The pavilion, bar and scorebox were all surrounded with flowers and the ground was surrounded by hills, rather like a secret ground. The Valley of Peace was significant because no ladies are allowed to attend to support or spectate, this rule was only waived once at the fiftieth anniversary. Due to its size, sixes are fours and fours are twos. Henry Blofeld wrote a story about it in one of his books.

During the week, one of the I.Zingari team held a party at their lovely home, Mike and Winsome Dormer are the most hospitable people you can find in cricket. Later Mike, together with others, started The Willows Cricket Club, to support New Zealand youth and have achieved great success in that part of the world fostering the game, amongst their team were the whole Hadlee family of Walter, the patriarch of New Zealand cricket, Sir Richard his famous son and brothers Dale and Barry. They did our man the great honour of making him an overseas honorary life member.

At the end of the week the Auckland team flew back to their home city in the North Island, Bert Sutcliffe and Norma had again been with them. It was now an opportunity to visit Eden Park. Staying with the Captain and his family, Rowly and Sue Potter and their two daughters Natalie and Melanie, for the following week, they arranged for their guest to play three matches whilst in Auckland, one for the Cricket Society, who had David Crowe in their side, father of the brilliant Martin and Jeff, who captained New Zealand.

One, for the University Old Boys – known as the Fingletoads, this team was run by Peter McDermott, the New Zealand representative on the ICC.

The match was played on the beautiful university grounds. The last match was outside Auckland on the day he was to fly back to England, he played for Auckland Police, only just making the flight through the police driving at over a hundred kph, reaching the airport with minutes to spare.

As he was their guest he was flying first class with all the trimmings, however, on arrival at Los Angeles the flight was fully booked, which should have meant he would be off loaded to the flight the following day.

This would have caused considerable inconvenience to him and the family at home, so he explained that he was a guest of the Airline and had been invited by the Managing Director, name dropping, so the Captain of the aircraft offered him his rest seat, situated at the back of the flight deck and all was well. The Captain and crew treated one as a VIP and champagne flowed throughout the flight, added to which, directly the plane cleared American air space, they supplied regular updates on the Test Match score and finally, the invitation came to watch the landing from the cockpit, for the approach to London Heathrow Airport, only returning to one's seat for the landing in thick snow! Was it only two weeks, it might have been a month; fun, hospitality galore and wonderful friendship. The New Zealanders made one Englishman feel like he had been adopted. This is the modus operandi of the Golden Oldies events.

John Davison and Gullivers Sports Tours had organised the travel and event with their normal efficiency and panache.

Bert Sutcliffe MBE
b. 23 November 1923 – d. 20 April 2001

By Rowly Potter
(Chairman of The Auckland Cricket Society)

Bert is considered by many knowledgeable cricket followers and supporters to be New Zealand's leading cricketer. Bert was an outstanding left-handed batsman, a very accomplished fielder and an interesting occasional orthodox left arm spin bowler. Bert was born in Ponsonby, Auckland. His parents had emigrated from Lancashire in 1921. Bert played his junior cricket at Point Chevalier Primary School going on to captain the Senior XI in 1934 and 1935. It was at Takapuna Grammar School where Bert really began to make a name for himself, scoring 113* in a junior house match. Here he won a place in the Senior XI and played for six seasons from 1937-38, the last three as captain. He scored 2,730 runs with an average of 71.8 and took 117 wickets at an average 11.5.

Bert represented Auckland Colleges in a one-day fixture against Sir Julian Chan's touring team in the 1938-39 season. The following season he was a member of the successful Auckland Brabin Cup team. In 1939-40 he started playing senior cricket for the Parnell Cricket Club, based at Eden Park, and in 1940-41 scored his first senior century. Other New Zealand players in that Parnell side were H.G. Vivian, P.E. Whitelaw and W.M. Wallace.

Bert's first class career then began in the 1941-42 season playing for Auckland against Wellington. This was the only first class fixture that season. His first class career finished in 1965-66. In all Bert played 233 first class matches, 407 innings, scored 44 centuries including triple and double centuries, and had a highest score of 385 for Otago against Canterbury in Christchurch in the 1952-53 season.

Bert played 42 Test matches. The first was against England at Lancaster Park, Christchurch in March 1947 where he scored 58 out of a total of 345 for 9 declared. His last Test innings was the first Test against England at Edgbaston, Birmingham, in May 1965. He scored 4 and retired hurt in the first innings, then scored 53 in the second innings.

Bert was the Sportsman of the Year in 1949 and was the Decade Champion for the 1940s for New Zealand.

Bert and Norma (nee Farrell) were married in 1948 on Bert's return from service overseas in Egypt, Italy and Japan as a sergeant with Infantry and Signals. He played in a number of cricket games while on war service. On returning to New Zealand he had a most rewarding season for Auckland. The next season he played for Otago, then came back to Auckland before returning to Otago for eleven consecutive seasons, the last four as captain.

Bert and Norma had three children, Christine, Lynne and Gary. On returning to Auckland Bert worked for the Rothmans Foundation with Martin Horton coaching cricket. Outside of cricket, Bert and Norma were very keen card players with family cards evenings held one night a week. Fishing, golf and then bowls were other favourite pastimes of Bert, while Norma was rarely without her knitting. Bert was a more than a useful exponent at hanging wallpaper.

Auckland Cricket Society

Bert was a member of the Auckland Cricket Society in the early days when the clubrooms were situated next to the main ground at Eden Park.

Then in 1994 the Auckland Cricket Society elected Bert as their President, a position that he held until 2001.

Bert was elected the fourth Life Member of the Society in 1998.

Bert was more than just a figurehead as President. During his time the Society played a number of games on the Outer Oval at Eden Park. During these fixtures Bert was the drinks carrier and barman. Visiting teams delighted in meeting Bert and having friendly discussions with him, especially about cricket.

I was very fortunate to have Bert as our President during my time as Chairman of the Cricket Society. He provided wise counsel at meetings and good advice at other times when asked.

Golden Oldies Cricket

Early in 1984 the first Air New Zealand Golden Oldies Cricket Festival was held in Auckland. The Cricket Society entered three teams, all captained by previous New Zealand captains, Barry Sinclair, Bevan Congdon and Bert Sutcliffe. The Sinisters, all left-handed batsmen, including John Edrich from England, had Bert as their skipper. The first playing day of the festival had all the teams at the Auckland Domain for the festival welcome and then the games.

The second Golden Oldies Festival was held in Brighton, England in 1986. The full touring party was made up of 90 players, wives, and supporters. As one of the younger team members it was my first opportunity to get to know Bert and Norma. Before leaving for England regular practice was held in the indoor school at Eden Park and Bert generously gave coaching and batting advice which was very much appreciated.

Arriving in London, England Bert was busy meeting up with friends and acquaintances from his 1949 tour and also giving interviews. The England-New Zealand Test took place at The Oval on 21st August and Bert arranged for those members of our party who were interested to attend the match. Bert was a guest of Raman Subba Row for the day. We witnessed Ian Botham trapping Jeff Crowe lbw to become the leading wicket-taker in Test cricket with 356 wickets.

For the third game of the Festival, the Cricket Society played against an Australian team at the Cuckfield Cricket Club. That evening Cuckfield entertained them, and Bert played the piano with many sing-a-long favourites. Bert had been a regular on the piano in the evenings during his tours with the New Zealand team.

In 1988 the Golden Oldies Festival was held in Brisbane, Australia. The Cricket Society started with a pre festival tour in Sydney and then travelled onto Brisbane, stopping and playing three games on the way. The first match was against The Primary Club against a number of ex Australian players. Bert, as our team leader, wore a cap which proclaimed "I'm their leader, which way did they go".

Vancouver, Canada, was the venue for the 1990 Festival. Bert and Norma were in attendance and gave their support to the Cricket Society teams. A highlight was playing at the Oak Bay Cricket Club on Vancouver Island against Cuckfield Cricket Club. With much encouragement from Bert the Society had a win on this occasion.

Bert was the Festival Ambassador for the 2000 Festival held in Rotorua, New Zealand. All teams at some time during the festival had Bert watch their progress as he visited all the game venues.

Harry Solomons
The largest cricket sports retailer in the world

By Hamesh Solomons

Harold Lindsay Solomons was always bound to succeed at just about everything he turned his hand to doing. I guess we could assume that somewhere in his tough Ceylonese upbringing it was bred into him. He was born in 1947, and sadly a few years later he lost his young mother, who died during childbirth with her fourth son at the tender age of just 21.

Harold cut his teeth in boarding school, where conditions were more spartan than merely a little rough and tumble. After school he was forced to join the plantation industry and it was during this period that times became very harsh for those not of native Ceylonese blood. Harry himself was of 'Dutch Burgher' ancestry and during the insurgence, he and his ilk had no better option than to pack up and start new lives as paupers in countries such as Australia, England, America and Canada.

As it would turn out, Harry brought his young wife and one year-old child to Sydney, where he worked as a prison guard as a first job. He arrived in the country with about 150 Australian dollars and five smuggled Sieko watches which he sold at a profit to keep his young family going.

The determination, passion and tenacity that would become the lifeblood of Harry's being were demonstrated through an experience early in his career at Long Bay Gaol. Harry was locking up when he was "King Hit" by an escaping prisoner, shattering his nose over his face. Not wanting to fail in the line of duty, Harry fought off the violent offender and held onto his keys with so much determination that the key tag penetrated through one of his fingers.

Perhaps this served as an early indication that Harry needed eventually to find a new and more enjoyable line of work, but for the time being he would do his job really well and move up the ranks quickly in the Corrective Service system.

Digressing back to Harry's School days, it was, oddly enough, an Italian American jesuit priest who would make an enormous impact. It was this priest, Oliver Morelli, who introduced the game of cricket to a very young Solomons. I guess you can say from that moment on he never looked back. Showing a natural inclination for the game, Harry soon became a school star and went on to represent Ceylon Schoolboys against an English XI and other zonal teams in Sri Lanka.

Cricket became everything to Solomons. Sadly, however, he had to relinquish any thoughts of serious senior cricket due to his new job on the plantations. As we would find out though, the passion within would never die.

Coming to Australia with little more than a few dollars in his wallet, Harry found himself living in Kingsgrove, a working class suburb in Sydney of established white Australians and immigrants from, in the main, Greece and Italy. It was here he found that the local sports store was for sale.

Going into partnership with his older brother, Markie, he managed to muster up some money to buy the tiny business and thus the story of Australia's most famous cricket business was born.

Through its early beginnings, Harry continued to work at Long Bay Gaol whilst the store was managed by his then wife, Frankie. However, as the business developed and other opportunities arose, Harry brought down the curtain on his prison days.

One such opportunity came by way of a travelling Indian businessman named Dips Banergee, who was on the look-out for someone to take on his Indian cricket brand, Symonds, in Australia. This was a challenge that Harry could not resist and a pivotal moment in his business career for it was in this new role that Harry was to flourish as an entrepreneur. Importantly, it also allowed him to get his foot in the door to the all-important Australian and international cricket arena.

Harry also met Christopher Bazalgette at this time. Chris was managing Gordon Greenidge, a player Harry regarded highly and needed in the Symonds stable. Harry got his wish.

As the new leader of the Symonds brand in their tough foray into the Australian cricket market, Harry's first coup was the signing of a cricket legend, Doug Walters, who also became an employee of the newly formed company. He has a hundred Dougie stories to relate from the times the two of them travelled the length and breadth of Australia introducing the Symonds brand.

Within a short period of time, Harry had successfully transformed the Symonds brand into a major player alongside the established names such as Gray-Nicolls, Slazenger, Gunn & Moore and County.

On his books now were the likes of Mark Taylor, Peter Toohey, Dirk Wellham, Michael Slater, Len Pascoe, Mike Whitney, Allan Border, Greg Matthews, Steve Smith, Terry Alderman, Graham Yallop, Trevor Barsby and John McGuire - among a whole host of others.

It was during this period that Harry chanced upon a young family from south-west Sydney. Here was not just one talented young cricketer but a set of amazingly gifted twins. Harry took a gamble and sponsored both the young boys. They were the Waugh boys, Steve and Mark. He soon became a friend to the Waugh family and a mentor of sorts to them both.

It was at this time that Christopher Bazalgette became a

useful contributor to the cricketing careers of the Waugh twins. Through Harry, Christopher arranged for the twins to gain their first experience in English cricket with contracts to play in the Lancashire League. This was a milestone in their young careers.

Harry did all he could to encourage, mentor and support the boys as they rose rapidly through the cricketing ranks. He even had them working at the Kingsgrove sports shop on a part-time basis and managed their equipment contracts free of charge.

Besides the Waugh twins, Harry also continued to venture into mentoring and sponsoring other young, up-and-coming cricketers such as Mark Taylor, Greg Matthews, Brad McNamara and stars such as Larry Gomes, Malcolm Marshall, Courtney Walsh, Gordon Greenidge (West Indies), Imran Khan, Qasim Omar, Mohin Khan, Abdul Qadar (Pakistan), Aravinda de Silva, Duleep Mendes, Roy Dias (Sri Lanka), Mohammad Azharuddin, Roger Binny and K Srikanth (India). To name but a few.

As the reputation of the players, such as Doug Walters, the Waugh twins, Allan Border, Mark Taylor, grew . . . so did the stature and the legend of Harry Solomons and Kingsgrove Sports Centre around Australia and throughout the cricket world.

The first creation was Kingsgrove Cricket Academy at Harry's head office – it is considered by many to be the first full-time cricket academy in Australia, maybe in the world. This was but a part of his new cricketing vision for Kingsgrove Sports Centre which also includes a large cricket store, warehouse and museum.

Then came his first Kingsgrove outlet in the western area of Sydney. There followed five further outlets around Sydney and in New South Wales.

It is common knowledge that no visit to Sydney or Australia

by any managing director or CEO of any cricket brand or cricket manufacturer is complete without a visit to Harry's Kingsgrove head office. No new project or development of cricket gear is started without consultation and discussion with Harold Lindsay Solomons. His influence in cricket circles in Australia spreads far and wide among cricketers and administrators alike.

If one should be in interested in cricket memorabilia and cricket nostalgia, a visit to see Harry's collection at his museum is a 'must do'. Unfortunately, space in his museum is limited and some of his best and oldest items are hidden away in his office, boardroom or in storage. A new purpose-built museum is in the planning stage and we can expect it to be a wonderful showcase for what is considered to be one of the best private collections in the world.

CHAPTER 5

Borat from the Ali G Show

Creation, preservation and Innovation

B ack in UK, *The Cricketer* was having another good year
and articles and advertisement sales were proceeding well.
It was a warm summer and it was as usual fairly energetic on
all fronts. Broadhalfpenny Down and The Bat & Ball Inn
were another of our man's haunts as he played for The
Broadhalfpenny Brigands and nearby Hambledon, who used
the ground on historic occasions. Therefore it was not
surprising for the current publican, Bill Galbraith, to ask him
to help found a new cricket club under the banner of The Bat
& Ball, which at the time was owned by Ind Coope, the
brewers. Their regional manager had the misjudgement to
endeavour to change this 'Shrine to English cricket', into the
new name of 'Natterjacks' an almost extinct toad.

From a marketing viewpoint it was perfect, our man's
cricketing contacts supported the new club from all around
the world. Celebrities went on television, others wrote letters
to the press and the owners; radio and papers rallied to the
cause, there was uproar and The Bat & Ball Cricket Club had
238 members and was launched on 1st February 1993. The
ethos of the club was to keep the Inn associated with cricket
'in perpetua' and support the playing of the game on
Broadhalfpenny Down, whilst raising money for youth
cricket.

The club colours were light blue and white, following the colours of the original Hambledon club that played on the ground in the eighteenth century. Leslie Thomas, author, wit and cricket fanatic agreed to honour the club by being its first President. Each year several high profile matches would be played. Brian Johnston the cricket commentator, humourist and television and radio broadcaster wrote and went on radio saying 'I will never drink the brewery's beer again'. Sadly he never did, because within a few days he became ill and died.

Later Coope sold the Inn to the local brewers – George Gale & Sons and The Bat & Ball Inn remained safe.

In this, their first season the new club hosted another beneficiary, Tim Tremlett with his Hampshire team-mates, the result being that Tim raised a good return for his benefit and the club made money for youth cricket.

The Bat & Ball Inn, relived days of old when it catered for all the spectators.

At this time he was contacted by an Australian television company who were producing a programme on club cricket and its origins in England for distribution in Australia, North America and Europe. Our man provided copy, interviews and historical data for Beyond Publications.

It was shown on the History wavelength in UK and during a Test Match lunch interval in Perth a few years later.

1994 was a bowling landmark, during the match between the Hampshire Hogs and Eton Ramblers he took his 751st wicket so bettering the previous career record of 750 held by the late Francis Irving.

In 1995 the Hampshire County Club named itself as the beneficiary and as they had had so many successful days with our organiser, asked him to arrange a special day on 'The Down', this match would be in-conjunction with the Broadhalfpenny Brigands, who held the lease to the ground, from the owners' Winchester College.

A special joint Committee was set up and it was agreed that instead of the club members providing the opposition, the Bat & Ball CC would be represented by Test and County cricketers – the result was that Malcolm Marshall captained the team, Gus Logie, Phil Simmons, Alvin Kallicharan and Roger Harper, all West Indies Test cricketers played, together with the brilliant former England left arm spinner, 'Deadly' Derek Underwood, (later to become MCC President in 2009),Peter Graves star batsman from Sussex, Ian Pont from Essex, Viv Pike who was to play for Gloucestershire, Rupert Cox (Hampshire) and Jonathan Grant who was 12th man and played when David Gower was unavailable at the last moment. A special programme was published carrying articles from: the doyen of cricket writers' John Woodcock of The Times, Mark Nicholas and Ivo Tennant were other contributors. Roger Vernier organised the Corporate Hospitality and a great day was spent raising around £5000 from some 2000 spectators and supporting businesses. All the local media, press, radio and television were fulsome in support and the late Major Tim Bible ran the raffle with over a hundred prizes. The Broadhalfpenny Brigands joined with Bat & Ball members to make the day run smoothly. The Bat & Ball Inn 'Mine Hosts' Dick and Lesley Orders were extremely supportive and coped with all the catering for the multitude of spectators, just as his predecessor John Nyren would have done two centuries before.

The winter before, Sandals, the West Indies' holiday resorts' company, invited their press agency, Compass Marketing, to hold a press conference in Antigua prior to the West Indies tour, the following summer to England. Sally Allen, their Managing Director, invited our man to provide the team members' profiles and write the press releases for the tour. This included writing the data for the press conference in Antigua and visiting the island for one week, taking the thirty strong World Press journalists to meet the Sandals' executives on the island.

This was an unprecedented situation that an Advertisement Manager, admittedly one who wrote features, was providing his editorial team and the Press worldwide with the original copy, had they been aware they would have been horrified, the tour coverage would definitely received less reportage. Editors and journalists feel that the word 'Advertising' is only just an acceptable necessity.

Therefore, if you can imagine the situation when they all met at Heathrow Airport on the Sunday morning, most of the World cricket press knew each other, but our man only knew a few of them. So, when a voice behind him said 'I don't know whether you would remember me, but I met you when you were looking after Ian Botham', those journalists that heard were amazed, for they could see who it was – none other than Viv Richards later to become Sir Vivian. He had recognised the back view of our man. The word quickly spread that this organiser was not just an administrative lightweight, but someone who had the right connections.

It was just the answer to one's prayers to 'break the ice'.

On arrival in Antigua there was an interesting situation, Sandals is a special resort for romantic honeymoon couples, so you can imagine the funny looks that were received when thirty men arrived together!!!

They had been allocated a completely new building, however, the arrival had been planned that even before unpacking, there was a champagne party. The Sandals complex is on the north western coast of the island, with a lagoon in which there is a bar, bars are free as, all food and drinks are normally part of the all-in cost of the holiday, the whole party were guests of Sandals. In each of the rooms there was a tray of bottles including champagne, rum, whisky, Gin and port plus all soft drinks and mixers in each fridge. If a drink was taken from any bottle it would be replaced with a new bottle the following morning. Similarly, if one met someone beside the bar and you went off for a swim your glass would be replenished on your return. There were two Jacuzzis in front of our building and three different restaurants on the complex. Other amusements such as golf, sailing, swimming, tennis and water skiing were also available. During the visit Australia were the visiting touring team playing a Test Match in the nearby St John's Cricket ground. Apart from the Press Conference, which took up one morning, as the organisers the remainder of the time was leisure. The cricketing journalists were reporting the Test Match for their papers.

The complete party were due to fly back to the UK on the following Monday and on the Sunday evening, Butch Stewart who flew in, a surprise visit from the Sandals owner, in his private jet from Jamaica. He told everyone that he was flying down to St Lucia the following morning. Anybody wishing to join him would be most welcome. Some of the journalists stated they would need to file their reports, but he answered this, by saying he would send the jet back for them later. There would not be a problem, as they would be able to fly back in the evening to Antigua, to catch their flight to England. So it was a flight in a private jet to St Lucia early next morning, a meeting with Butch Stewart and a conducted tour of the island and some breakfast at the St Lucia Sandals.

Our man went with *The Mirror* Sports Editor for a round of golf, buggies and caddies of course and clubs made available. On our return to the club house, a car was waiting to return to Sandals hotel for lunch and meeting with the second wave who had come down later. One little occurrence that shows the company's attention to detail, whilst going round the St Lucia Sandals our man bought some cigarettes and the shop did not have enough change and by the time they re embarked for the flight back to Antigua he had forgotten all about it. On their return they had to settle their accounts and when he came to pay, he was advised that his bill was less the change that was owed from the other island. Just to put the 'icing on the cake', Sandals had put on a special lobster supper for the whole party before they loaded their bus for the airport. This week was organised by their Sales Director - Donald Roper, nobody would have questioned his brilliant arrangements, quiet efficiency and professionalism, nothing was ever too much trouble and everything went to plan. Two frequent visitors were Wes Hall and Andy Roberts, who were the Coach and Manager of the West Indian tour to the UK and it was in their interest to know the Press party before they arrived in England.

The following year he was made an Honorary Life member of The Crusaders Cricket Club, who are based in Melbourne, Australia – for his services to cricket.

The Cricketer was at its best at this time and business was good on all quarters, our man was very busy, every year besides selling advertisements he also wrote the world equipment supplement, two ground equipment features, attended exhibitions and smaller articles amounting, in all, to around fifty thousand words. In 1997 one of the wooden sight screens at the Hampshire Hogs ground rotted, he had a brainwave that amounted to designing a screen that would have a base of galvanised iron, therefore not likely to rust, and a roller at the base with a white mesh nylon which would be wound up from its base like when you raise a sail up the mast. When the match was not in process the rewind would occur and the rolled up screen could be locked in a box away from vandals. He knew a company that already had a galvanised surround and the mesh screen. As he had played cricket whilst at school, against the Managing Director, he believed they would not abuse his trust, the upshot was the Retrax screen was

Above: The author playing his last official match.

Above: Robin Smith, Hampshire's prolific batsman and Captain, who was hugely successful for England, Robin spoke at the Author's Benefit Dinner.

Above: The 10th Duke of Richmond and Gordon's team, together with The Lord's Taverners, when they played to mark the Tri-centenary of cricket at Goodwood in 2002.

designed, but in their wisdom they decided to put the roller at the top. They gave him a royalty on all sales. The screens sold well and gained the authority of being used on the Nursery ground at Lords. Everything went well until the father retired and then the Royalty was discontinued.

His next venture followed a year later, he had taken up golf, first playing right handed and this was progressing well, until he found the strain on his damaged left knee was too great, so he reverted to playing left handed, this was not that hard as he is a left handed batsman. He was surprised how many people played golf. So he put it to the Hampshire Hogs that he should start a golf section to raise funds for their youth cricketers, it was agreed and this section has now had fifty events 2008, raising a healthy two thousand pounds per year. He has a small committee and has been ably helped by Christopher Van der Noot, who he first met when they were both eleven.

His daily activity selling advertisements brought him into contact with many former County and Test cricketers such as Bob Taylor, the England & Derbyshire wicket-keeper, Bob Cook (Essex), Colin Cowdrey (Kent & England), Richard Hutton (Yorkshire & England), Devon Malcolm (Derbyshire and England), Jack Russell (Kent & England), John Snow (Sussex and England), Fred Rumsey (Somerset, Derbyshire and England), amongst others. Colin Cowdrey, later to become Lord Cowdrey of Tonbridge, and Richard Hutton were Directors of *The Cricketer*. The others either worked for or provided cricket products or services, which they advertised in *The Cricketer* International.

One very special cricketer he met on many occasions was the one and only Sir Garry Sobers, probably the greatest ever all-rounder, the former Nottinghamshire and West Indies Captain, who, batting left-handed could take any attack apart, being particularly harsh on spin bowlers. He also excelled as a bowler, he bowled left arm – spin, medium paced cutters and fast medium swing. When he retired he became a good golfer, with a dry sense of humour.

Another was the great Alec Bedser (Surrey and England) who was the guest speaker at a Dinner *The Cricketer* held at the Belfry hotel, nr. Birmingham, after the event our man chauffeured him back to London.

Alec believed that bowlers learnt their art by bowling and bowling and bowling. He said 'If you bowl line and length the ball can either move a little off the seam, or alternatively, if you swing it slightly one way or other, you will be a valuable asset to your team, AND you will take many wickets'. It was great advice, by playing a lot and practising your art, the experience will always bear fruit.

To mark the turn of a new Century *The Cricketer* decided to hold a special international cricket Festival for wandering cricket clubs, the event was held on the Oxford University grounds and teams were put up in the various Halls of residence. Teams came from Holland, South Africa, America and joined with the county club sides from all parts of England.

Each team would play three matches and the event ended with a special Dinner.

Our man was part of the organising operation and would also participate for The Hampshire Hogs, in the week prior to the Festival Christopher Martin-Jenkins, editor of *The Cricketer* and chief cricket journalist for The Times, represented the Free Foresters in a match against The Hogs. At the time he was nearing a thousand wickets for the Hogs, and for some matches including this one failed to take a wicket. CMJ now wrote a piece for The Times on the forthcoming Festival and mentioned our man's hoped-for target describing his cricket as follows 'When he runs in the field he runs at the same pace as The Queen Mother (who was a hundred at the time), and when he bowls – batsmen self destruct'. Christopher Martin-Jenkins obviously had a large readership, for in the next three days our man took twelve wickets, leaving him three wickets short of the thousand.

The launch of the Festival kept everyone of the organisers very busy on the first morning, matches started at noon and our man's match was against De Flamingoes from Holland, unknown to him the Hog's organiser John Bristow had advised Tim Brocklehurst, *The Cricketer*'s head man about the possibility of the landmark being reached. Hence when our man was introduced into the attack the champagne was on ice.

He took his first wicket with his first ball, next man in wasn't long before he skied one, watching from the other end was Henk Moll, the then Dutch No. 4, a powerful young batsman and on facing this slow bowler he decided he should be put in his place – the first ball was hit wide of long off, the next went over long on, who misjudged it and it went over his arms for four. But the next ball was hit to the safe hands of Rupert Preece and Henk Moll became part of The Hampshire Hogs history. The game stopped and champagne was passed around. The Festival was a great success and everyone enjoyed the occasion.

Christopher Martin-Jenkins comments in The Times provided the catalyst for our man to branch out into writing his first commercial book.

The fact was that bowling slowly, in all its various forms; off spin, leg spin, chinaman and googly, floaters and swing, reverse swing combined with flight and guile are a major science that few have ever mastered.

Seldom do you here a bowler talk about trajectory, which this student believes is probably the most important and every batsman will succumb to a certain trajectory, how to gauge which, is the secret, because several factors must be considered: the experience and quality of the batsman, his height and fitness, his judgement of ball length and desire to hit the ball.

Most cricketers only touch on the subject. It is not unlike a spider weaving his web for the unsuspecting insect, or the fishermen deciding which fly and then casting across the flowing river.

First was the need to find out if there was a niche in the market that had not been written about, there are many coaching books describing 'How to Bowl or Bat' including equipment, the way to stand, and how to hold the ball. But there was NOT any book covering the mental approach, probably the most important area, as, if you can master your opponent mentally, then even his greater ability will be diminished. Initially our man thought he would only write on SLOW BOWLING, but then he thought 'Why not write on all aspects of the mental approach?

He consulted the expert exponents, his friend Derek 'Deadly' Underwood the greatest left-arm spin bowler, arguably of all time, as bowling left-arm was a very different approach, but Deadly only described bowling at people like Sir Donald Bradman. This book would be aimed at amateur cricketers, emphasizing the learning curve for the younger reader. The man who was eventually chosen was his great friend John Appleyard, whose prowess was well known to all those who had played in *The Cricketer* Cup over four decades, together with Minor Counties as he played for Hertfordshire over 18 years and Captained the County for seven years. John was ideal as his wide experience provided knowledge on all sections of the subject and agreed to become a Joint author. Apart from the play already stated he had Captained Guernsey and Malta and is an advanced coach. John became more involved to the extent he agreed to become co-author, this was a great help, as many would criticise one person's opinion but not two authors. The book was written in three months and illustrations were gathered (it was decided they should be humerous), this was one of the hardest tasks. Once the book was finished a publisher had to be found. Neither author had the experience of finding a publisher, although our man's experience with journal publishing gave him a range of contacts, which he now proceeded to trawl.

One Publisher told him it would take a year to publish, that was no good as he wanted it on the market within three months. However, a former acquaintance, Michael Massey – the previous Northern Sales Manager for the IPC group had moved on and now worked with Empire Publications, he said they published books and to send him the manuscript, this was done and a week later they agreed to publish. John Appleyard came up with the name – THINK Cricket – Compete Mentally. Robin Smith, the then Hampshire and England cricketer, who also captained Hampshire CCC agreed to write the Foreword and David Money edited the final draft.

Michael Massey was the contact with Empire and he worked tirelessly to bring the book together and it was published prior to the start of the 2001 cricket season. Initially our man was given a great honour by The Hampshire Hogs, as they gave him a luncheon recognising the fact that the season before he had reached a thousand wickets for the club.

At the luncheon he launched the book and sold 120 copies, this was followed the next day by a Book Launch at The Bat & Ball Inn, courtesy of Mr and Mrs Dick Orders, landlords of the famous Inn. A further 200 copies were distributed to the press and public. One of the leading cricket journalists was Robin Marlar, who later became Chairman of Sussex CCC. This later venture required great energy from the author, for Publishers only promote books for around six months, so with his worldwide contacts he now had to develop the market. He gained the endorsement of The New Zealand Coaching Board, Ali Bacher as Managing Director of South African cricket bought copies, the Lords shop and all the first class County cricket shops helped to sell the publication. Aware of the risk the book might be copied he delayed sales to India and Pakistan till a year later. He then gained an Indian, J.K. Mahendra, who achieved about 700 sales. The web was another useful outlet and seven years later the book – *THINK Cricket* has almost sold out, just over 5000 copies.

Needing a new impetus for the book to have its first reprint he looked for another publisher and found a company called Green Umbrella, who offered to take the book into their stable.

However, to return to 2001, two months after his first book launch his daughter married Sebastien in Reading. It was two years earlier they had met and just prior to meeting his future parents in law, Seb had returned from an evening out with his girlfriend and they turned on their television. To my daughter's amazement – as they watched a new show 'Ali Gee', suddenly Borat from Kazakhstan was being introduced to cricket in an interview with her father. Seb was due to meet her father at lunch the following day!!

Borat had met and been shown cricket ten months earlier, introduced as a foreign correspondent, in full make-up. Nobody explained it was a set-up, the meeting lasted some three hours. Borat's opening question was 'Did cricketers due to play a match rape and pillage their opponents the night before?' This set the scene. Later he wanted to hold a bat and all the party moved to Broadhalfpenny Down where a Ladies match was in progress. As the day progressed the questions became more and more obscure, thus our man decided if it was a wind-up you needed a straight man and this would be his role. Apart from its first showing, it was then repeated the following evening, then later in the year. The comedian became very popular and the programme was repeated many times in different media. A film was made and it was put on youtube:

http://www.youtube.com//watch?v=txfHVG3ioAs

> Ali G: *When Cambridge students do not study, they like to play English game of cricket. I learn to play please. Thank you.*
> Christopher: *You're left handed, so you hold it with your top hand round there and your bottom hand there and when you...when the ball comes... now hit... have your feet further apart. Hold your bat there and when the ball comes... Watch me! watch me! You pick the ball... bat there... put your front forward foot...your f-f-front foot... right foot forward. Alright?*
> They underarm a ball to Borat who makes a half hearted attempt at blocking it with the bat.
> Christopher: *That's alright. Can, can I just show you something.*
> Borat: *Why do you touch me so much?*
> Chris: *No, now...now just pick up the bat there.*
> Borat kicks the ball away.
> Chris: *No, no, no, leave the ball there...no I want the ball to be there. No leave the ball alone! Up with the bat and out to the ball. Could you try and do that?*
> Borat: *Yes no problem.*

Chris: *No! Hands the other way round. That's right. What did I do?...* (Borat tries to imitate) *No I didn't! There! No. No, no, no you can't... Just do this... alright?*

Borat: *Let me!*

Chris: *Watch. There, that's all I want you to do.*

Borat: *Okay.*

Chris: *All you have to do... Now now put your foot there... and the bat comes down like that. But this foot should be over here. Your foot.* (tries to move Borat's leg which Borat subbornly keeps planted) *That's where the ball should be. And then you put there... but bend this there. The ball wont be standing still, it will bounce here and come up from there and that's a good shot.*

Borat (innocently): *And what do I do here?*

Christopher Martin-Jenkins MBE

By Christopher Bazalgette

It could be said that CM-J, as he is always known, missed perfection by one run.

Whilst captain of cricket at Marlborough he scored 99 at Lord's against Rugby. He had already decided what his profession was going to be, having written to Brian Johnston for advice on 'How to become a commentator'. He then went up to Fitzwilliam College, Cambridge, and read history for his degree.

He started his journalistic career with *The Cricketer*, under the guidance of E.W. 'Jim' Swanton, as assistant editor. After three years on general sports duties at the BBC he started commentating for Test Match Special in 1972 and has been a part of the team every summer and most winters ever since. He was appointed cricket correspondent in succession to Johnston in 1973. Weary of touring every winter, and with three young children to help look after, he opted out of this at the end of 1980 and returned to *The Cricketer* as editor in the magazine's Diamond Jubilee year, 1981. In 1984 the BBC persuaded him to resume duties as cricket correspondent and for the next six years he combined these with overall responsibility for *The Cricketer* as editorial director.

He also undertook some Test, and, more often, Sunday League, commentaries for BBC television but in 1990 he accepted an offer to become cricket correspondent of the Daily Telegraph, making a sufficient reputation for The Times to 'poach' him as their correspondent in 1999. He retired from regular newspaper writing in 2008. His journalistic output is one to be admired, for he has written some 20 books, including The Complete Who's Who of Test Cricketers.

These are some of the statistics about this amazing man, who has packed so much into his adult life. Everything CM-J wrote or has spoken has been meticulously researched and prepared. Although you might disagree with his opinion, you could find little to fault in his commentary. Unlike some modern reporters, his writing is always impeccable English grammar. A mild tempered man with a pleasant sense of humour, never using his wit to ridicule his subject, he replies personally to every letter received.

As a cricketer he played for the Marlborough Blues, The Arabs, MCC, Free Foresters, Surrey Young Amateurs and the county second X1, plus three clubs in the locality of his various homes in the Surrey/Sussex area, Cranleigh, Albury and Horsham. Recognition by your peers is something special. CM-J was chairman of The Cricket Writers Club from 1991 to 1993, Sports Reporter of the Year in 1996, and has added voluntary roles such as becoming a trustee of the Arundel Cricket Foundation and The Brian Johnston Memorial Trust. He was president of The Cricket Society from 1998 to 2008 and is now a vice president.

Most of these accolades would be enough for some, but Christopher has developed his speaking talents to reach the top echelon of 'After Dinner Speakers'. In 2007 MCC invited him to give 'the Cowdrey Lecture,' the first non-Test cricketer to do so. Public speaking apparently came with relative ease to someone who acted at Marlborough, where he once played the title role in John Osborne's Luther. Mimicry is another of his attributes; we are led to believe that he was forgiven for impersonating members of staff including 'the Master'. At Cambridge he progressed to writing and performing satirical skits for Footlights concerts, later sharing a double act with his younger brother, Timothy. His after dinner speeches may include various politicians, radio personalities or even fellow commentators in his repertoire.

That is the public face of CM-J. On the private front, he was consoled for missing the cricket blue he might have gained at Cambridge by meeting Judy, his lovely future wife, who has been his strong arm whilst he toured around the world as commentator. They have two boys – James, the elder, Robin who has now retired from playing cricket for Sussex- and a daughter, Lucy. CM-J is a competitive man. He plays tennis and golf, never having the time to practise, but you would rather have him on your side than against you.

His crowning glory was that he was appointed Member of The Order of The British Empire (MBE) in the 2009 New Year Honours and was chosen to become president of MCC for 2010-2011.

Author's Note:

I met Christopher when he was editor and later editorial director of *The Cricketer* International. Not only was his advice sound, he was helpful in introductions and always generous when polishing the editorial copy I submitted. He was also someone who would put the magazine first. Advertisers who booked at the last moment could make the difference between profit and loss, so having an editor who would give a page of editorial over to advertising was considerate indeed.

It was his inspiration that spurred me into writing my first book 'THINK-Cricket' and also he supported me in including six pages of my thoughts on the future of county cricket in his book 'Twenty Years On.'

CM-J has always been a man in a hurry. He has tried to pack 30 hours into each day and 70 minutes into each hour, which is the reason he is sometimes delayed for a meeting and even for his commentary session! But he would be the first to leave, rushing to the next event. If you telephone him, he will speak with you if he is there, but he will probably just be finishing an article for an imminent deadline. When playing cricket, if not on the field he will be replying to correspondence. But he will always make time for a friend and help if within his power. In 40 years, often under pressure, I have never known him discourteous or lose his temper.

Derek Underwood

By Christopher Bazalgette

Derek Leslie Underwood was born in Bromley, Kent, in 1945 and educated at Beckenham & Penge Grammar School. He made his first-class debut aged 17 and became the youngest bowler to take 100 championship wickets in his debut season. This was 1963 and he achieved the feat on ten occasions. In his career he gained one century - in his 591st match. But he was an excellent nightwatchman and could be relied on to stay in when those before him had failed.

He gained his first international cap at 21 against West Indies and only four years later celebrated taking his 100th Test wicket, whilst in the same year reaching 1,000 first-class wickets. In his Test career, he took 297 wickets at an average of 25.83, whereas his first class tally was 2,465 wickets at 20.28 per wicket. Given a sticky wicket (following rain) he was virtually unplayable.

In 1968 he took the last four Australian wickets in 27 balls to square the series and in 1970-71 dismissed Terry Jenner to regain the Ashes. In 1981 he was honoured with an MBE, playing his last Test match a year later, but not retiring until 1987. Since then, fame has been heaped on a man who was probably England's finest left arm bowler. He followed Godfrey Evans (Godders to his many friends who were members of El Vino's CC) as president of Antwerp CC in Belgium. 'Deadly' also honoured the author by becoming an honorary life member of The Bat & Ball CC in 1993. In !997 he was made patron of The Primary Club.

In 2004, Wisden's celebrated committee selected England's greatest post-war XI and Derek Underwood gained the left arm spinner's place. In 2006 he was made president of his county of Kent and in 2009 he was elected president of MCC. That same year he was made an honorary fellow of Canterbury Christ Church University and inducted into the ICC Cricket Hall of Fame, alongside Neil Harvey and Allan Border (Australia) and David Gower.

He is now chairman of The Stars Foundation for Cerebral Palsy. Although still working for Clubturf Cricket Ltd as sales director, Derek is finding more time for his other hobbies: he is a very competitive golfer and enjoys philately and music.

An Appreciation by Richard Merricks

Derek Underwood is, by anyone's standards, a remarkable cricketer. I have known him for the past 25 years or so, and have always found him a most delightful, modest and engaging person, as have most people who have followed the fortunes of Kent or English cricket.

Derek has been only the third bowler to become president of MCC (in spite of his pride in scoring his one first-class century at Hastings in 1984, he would not claim to be an all rounder, I don't think.) The other two, by the way, for quiz buffs, have been John Warr and Robin Marlar, rather more 'amateur-type' cricketers than the true professional.

Watching the combination of Derek and Alan Knott, as I did for so many years at Canterbury and other grounds, was to observe high levels of skill and artistry at both ends of the pitch – the gentle run in, the high arm action and the accuracy of the delivery was then matched by great powers of anticipation and smoothness from Knott, honed by many years experience of keeping to 'Deadly.'

Although Underwood was rather faster than the traditional left-arm spinner, he combined pin-point accuracy with the ability to turn the ball sharply, on occasions making it really "bite." This was of course enhanced when he bowled on uncovered wickets, as he did in the earlier part of his career, but after covering was introduced he was still a batsman's nightmare – hence the moniker 'Deadly' - especially in limited-overs matches when risks had to be taken.

In an interesting chapter called 'My Bowling Style' from his autobiography published in 1976, Derek recounts how such eminent judges as Les Ames and Colin Cowdrey tried to persuade him to bowl more slowly, or to deliver more balls from over the wicket.

All who were present at The Oval in 1968 – and many more besides – will remember Derek bowling out Australia to level the Ashes series after a thunderstorm had flooded the ground. The memory, and photograph, of Inverarity lbw Underwood, with less than five minutes to go, and nine English fielders clustered round the bat, remain etched on every cricket lover's mind.

Other remarkable performances were his 8-51 against Pakistan at Lord's in 1974, and in county cricket, 9-32 versus Surrey at The Oval in 1978, and 9-28 against Sussex on his favourite Hastings ground in 1964, a year after his debut. He was selected for World Series Cricket, but when one considers the quality of batsmen that he was confronting regularly in Test cricket – the Chappells, Sobers, Richards, Gavaskar, to name but a few – his records speak for themselves.

But, for all his prowess on the pitch, I think that it is as a gentleman, a genuinely popular opponent and a fine ambassador for the game of cricket that he will be most remembered.. He is sales director of a company providing artificial pitches and net surfaces to clubs and schools, which keeps him involved at grass-roots level.

Most ex-first-class cricketers are basically decent and friendly people who are quite happy to converse with their admirers but few do so, in my experience, in such an enthusiastic and whole-hearted way as Derek, who really makes you feel that your contribution is valuable, and comes over in such a genuine manner.

John Woodcock OBE

by Patrick Maclure

As they say in North West Hampshire: "Sage is to onions, as Woodcock is to Longparish." Rather surprisingly for Hampshire, the village in question lives up to its name, but the Patron of the Living does not and could indeed lay claim to being the most diminutive Patron in 'All England and Metropolitan', as well as in 'England and Metropolitan', just to show you that I may conceivably know more about archdioceses than the Patron himself, even though he occupies an Old Curacy.

But I digress.

In spite of the length of the parish, 'Wooders' is the best-known and most revered inhabitant, whose progress through the village either on foot plus stick, by car or motorised chariot, but mercifully no longer by Emmett-designed bicycle, is a slow process because he is frequently interrupted by men, women and children of all ages, not to mention dogs, ducks and birds - excluding herons who try to avoid him. He has served, and in several cases continues to serve, on every village committee, notably the Longparish Church Council, as well as being the most inveterate church-door-opener/locker, come snow, rain or shine. Anything worth knowing about local residents, or the village itself, can be gleaned over a pint in The Plough or a chat on the cricket-ground, which, thanks to his good offices, has seen a plethora of Test players performing there, perhaps most memorably Lord Cowdrey of Tonbridge, who having opened the village fête, wearing his England blazer, then allowed anyone to bowl six balls at him in a net for less than a pound.

As there have been Woodcocks, several of the cloth, involved with Longparish since the middle of the eighteenth century, it is not surprising that he is an iconic figure. When you add to the genealogical mix a great-uncle born in 1806, a grandfather in 1813 and a father in 1856, you can see that he comes from an unusual stable and that a diversity of gifts is unsurprising. He is, of course, a keen fisherman, as any Test-side resident must be, and has a beat on the Avon just to emphasise, as if it were necessary, that he is no snob. He knows most of what is worth knowing about shooting and he is the proud owner of a thatched house, readily identifiable to those approaching or leaving Thruxton aerodrome by the woodcock on the roof.

Returning to the Woodcock below the roof, it must be said that since youth he has suffered unfairly from physical discomforts which would have worn down most normal mortals, but a combination of unbreakable bones and unshakeable resolve, together with a determination to eschew self-pity, continues to see him through each succeeding torment. What he has endured at the hands of hip-surgeons fully entitles him to regular use of a hip-flask.

All of the foregoing is but a preface to a curriculum vitae of which the cricket world remains in awe. Born in 1926 and educated at the Dragon and St Edward's schools in Oxford, he then went further down the road to Trinity College, being awarded Hockey Blues in 1946 and 1947. After following England's 1951 tour of Australia with the BBC, he began his career in journalism the next season by joining the staff of the Manchester Guardian, moving on two years later as cricket correspondent of The Times, then under the editorship of Sir William Haley, where he remained in post until 1988; since then he has contributed articles for the paper on a regular basis, albeit not regularly enough for his many admirers, who appreciate his sagacity, succinctness and memorable turn of phrase and place him at the highest level in the Pantheon of cricket writers.

In addition he was the correspondent for Country Life for thirty seasons from 1962 and editor of Wisden from 1981 to 1986, being nominated as Sports Journalist of the Year in 1987. His publications comprised The Times One Hundred Greatest Cricketers, of which he was the sole author, The Ashes 1956, written jointly with Jim Swanton, and Barclays World of Cricket, for which he was Editor, in one manifestation or another, of its three editions. All in all, during a span of almost fifty years , he covered over forty Test tours, of which eighteen were to Australia. Consequently he knows every cricketer of note, with Sir Alec Bedser now heading the list, and most of those whom he does not know would love to know him. Hundreds of distinguished cricketers have received the ultimate tribute written by the supreme obituarist; I only hope that he has written his own!

He served on various sub-committees of the Marylebone Cricket Club, notably Arts and Library, where he remained for several lustra, as well as completing three terms on the main committee, followed by a period as a Trustee, after which he was deservedly elected a Life Vice President. His services to cricket were marked by his appointment as an Officer of the Order of the British Empire in 1996. In addition to being a member of almost all the well-known cricket clubs, except for some reason the Hampshire Hogs, he has been a lifelong member of St Enodoc Golf Club, which has enabled him to enjoy another game, to which he is devoted and upon which he has reported on a number of occasions.

His knowledge of cricket is constantly updated, as he continues to watch any match of consequence from his chair or, during the watches of the night, from his bed, whilst ensuring that he retains an independent opinion by having the volume knob almost invariably turned to zero.

Long may the Sage of Longparish continue to delight and

inform us with his pickings from 'the coarse cloth of memory and the silk of dreams.'

Robin Smith

by Andrew Renshaw

Word about the prodigious batting talent of Robin Smith reached us before his arrival at Hampshire, courtesy of his older brother. Chris was no mean batsmen himself – he averaged 45.63 for the county and played eight Tests – but he made it known that his kid brother, five years younger, would play many more times for England.

That did not absolve Robin from serving a long apprenticeship. Remarkably, he played 42 games for the second X1 from his first appearance in June 1981. This circuit was a dangerous place when Hampshire were playing. Back in 1973, Andy Roberts broke bones when he was qualifying; now Robin smashed windows with his big hitting.

In June 1983, Robin joined Chris in the team for his first county championship game, against Lancashire at Dean Park, Bournemouth. Chris, opening the batting, scored 100. Off the last ball of the day, Robin hit a boundary to bring up exactly 100 for his maiden first-class hundred. Altogether, Chris hit 47 centuries in his career, while Robin's final haul was 70. Big brother was right.

But Robin was soon back in the second team. His brief taste of life at the top only happened because Gordon Greenidge was away for a month playing in the World Cup. When Greenidge returned, Robin, still to qualify as an England player, had to drop down.

In Hampshire, 1984 was not so much the year of George Orwell but of Elvis. The man who kept Robin out of the first team for most of the season was Elvis Leroy Reifer. Signed as a one-year replacement for Malcolm Marshall, who was on international duties, the inexperienced Reifer, who had not played in a first-class match until he arrived in England, succumbed to fatigue in mid-August and gave way as the overseas player to Robin, who had just scored 132 and 97 against the Sri Lankan tourists.

Robin had to serve four years' qualification, so 1985 was his first summer as a fully-fledged England player. It was the first of four years of consolidation, marked by his top score in 1987 when he hit an unbeaten 209 against Essex at Southend – the only double century of his career. But while Hampshire fans recognised his potential, it took an innings of just 38 to bring him to national attention. This was a cameo at Lord's in the 1988 final of the Benson & Hedges Cup – the first time the county had found their way to NW8, 25 years after one-day competitions entered cricket's calendar. It sealed Hampshire's seven-wicket win, although they only had to overcome Derbyshire's total of 117. Robin stroked seven boundaries, including two in succession off Michael Holding, and impressed Richie Benaud in the TV commentary box.

Within a fortnight, Robin was making his Test debut at Headingley for an England team in crisis; this was Chris Cowdrey's only game as captain. Robin shared a century partnership with his fellow countryman Allan Lamb, making the same score (38) as in the B&H final. Against the West Indies quartet of Malcolm Marshall, Curtly Ambrose, Courtney Walsh and Winston Benjamin, Robin was given a baptism of fire which he countered with what was to become his hallmark: unflinching courage. A half century in the next Test at the Oval clinched his place, but did not save England from another defeat; it was their 18th Test without a win. Crisis time indeed. Fortunately, a one-off match against Sri Lanka allowed England to claim a victory when Robin struck the winning boundary.

From 1988 to 1996, Robin provided sterling service for England in 62 Tests. His highest score of 175 came at Antigua in 1994, although it gained little enough attention, as Brian Lara had just compiled 200 runs more, but it did allow England to match the West Indies total of 593.

How important was Robin's contribution to England? A look at the averages of his main contemporaries in the England batting line-up tells the story:

This is not the record of an under-achiever. Rather, it suggests that Robin's eight-year Test career should have been longer. The selectors did indeed cut it short. Robin also played in 71 one-day internationals in the same period from 1988 to 1996, with an average of 39.01 and a top score of 167 not out against Australia at Edgbaston in May 1993 – although he was on the losing side. It remains the highest score by an England player in ODIs. Of the 18 England players who like Robin (2,419) have scored more than 2,000 ODI runs, only two have an average in the 40s, Kevin Pietersen (fluctuating around 46) and Nick Knight (40.41).

Robin represented England before the introduction of central contracts, so he also played a lot of cricket for Hampshire. Having made a big impression at his first Lord's final in 1988, it was his innings there three years later that formed the centrepiece of what many of the county's supporters avow was their finest day. Hampshire went into the NatWest final against Surrey on September 7, 1991, having been rolled over that week at the Oval by the pace of Waqar Younis, who took 12 wickets in the match and broke the hand of skipper Mark Nicholas. Hampshire had already lost Chris Smith, who could no longer delay taking up a managerial post in Australia. Surrey scored 240 for five off their 60 overs, with Graham Thorpe making 93 and Alec Stewart 61. Tony Middleton, coming in for Chris Smith, opened for Hampshire in his first NatWest game and made 78. He was joined by Robin, who at first repelled Waqar and then counter-attacked in a compelling contest. As darkness fell, Jon Ayling struck a vital six but Robin was unluckily run out with two overs to go. Finally, Hampshire scraped home with two balls to spare. Robin not only won that match, but his scores in the preceding four games were 43*, 79*, 67 and 64*. They should have renamed it the Robin Smith Trophy.

	M	I	NO	Runs	HS	Ave	100	50	Strate
Graham Thorpe	100	179	28	6744	200*	44.66	16	39	43.89
David Gower	117	204	18	8231	215	44.25	18	3	50.59
Robin Smith	62	112	15	4236	175	43.67	9	28	43.65
Graham Gooch	118	215	6	8900	333	42.58	20	46	49.23
Alec Stewart	133	235	21	8463	190	39.54	15	45	48.66
Mike Atherton	115	212	7	7728	185*	37.69	16	46	37.31
Nasser Hussain	96	171	16	5764	207	37.18	14	33	40.38
Allan Lamb	79	139	10	4656	142	36.09	14	18	51.40
Mike Gatting	79	138	14	4409	207	35.55	10	21	43.15
Graeme Hick	65	114	6	3383	178	31.32	6	18	48.88
Mark Ramprakash	52	92	6	2350	154	27.32	2	12	36.18

Robin excelled on the big stage at Lord's. Earlier in 1991, he had taken a magnificent 148* off West Indies attack, and the following year, when Hampshire returned to headquarters for the B&H final, he hit 90 and took Hampshire to a hat-trick of knockout wins.

In 1996, Hampshire fans showed their appreciation by rewarding Robin with a then county record benefit of £202,000. Alas, most of the funds disappeared and he was granted a testimonial in 2003. By then he had captained the side for five years, from 1998 to 2002, and if the results were nothing special, he delivered much-needed consistency at a difficult time in the county's history as Hampshire moved from Northlands Road to the Rose Bowl. Robin, in any case, was an initial short of the tradition of Hampshire captains, notably EDR Eagar, ACD Ingleby-Mackenzie, RMC Gilliat, NEJ Pocock and MCJ Nicholas. (The honourable exception was the man who captained the county most times and who had just the two initials – Lord Tennyson.)

The pitches in the early years at the new ground did batsmen no favours, but Robin scored one typically courageous hundred in 2001 when he was peppered by a new generation of Australian fast bowlers. He led Hampshire to a famous victory – the county's first over Australia since the year the Titanic sailed out of Southampton. He was forced to miss the next match nursing sore ribs.

By the time Robin retired at the end of the 2003 season, he had scored 26,155 first-class runs, which places him at number 100 in the all-time list. Then add on his 14,927 one-day runs. But what really mattered was the style in which those runs came. The mind's eye will replay the cracking square cuts, the thumping cover drives and the powerful pulls and hooks. The heart will treasure above all Robin's bravery and his loyalty. Many will fondly share these memories because Robin remained throughout his 23-year career friendly and approachable.

Mark Nicholas summed up Robin's contribution by concluding that he was Hampshire's greatest cricketer, adding that he was "the most universally popular cricketer in the world game". Who would disagree?

Andrew Renshaw edited the Hampshire Handbook *from 1995 to 2008. He is a vice-president of Hampshire and president of Eversley CC.*

CHAPTER 6

Publishing

The Lady who Rules

One of his friend's had an annual cricket match against his village (one of the first ever cricket clubs: Peperharow CC). Prior to which they always have a lunch. On one such occasion they found on arrival cameras set up - the friend Jumbo Fuller is known as a great practical joker, so everyone was very wary, but on this occasion it was genuine as, Jumbo lived in Bentley village and this village life was featured weekly in a programme called 'The Village'. The lunch and ensuing cricket match was filmed and put out the following week. This programme was also repeated on other channels several times.

THINK Cricket needed to be marketed and this was done firstly, by arranging for all the County cricket grounds who had shops to stock it, including all the main Test Match grounds – Lords, The Kennington Oval, Trent Bridge, Edgbaston, Old Trafford and Headingly. Now it was time to look further afield, New Zealand were first to respond, their Coaching section endorsed the book. Australia was unable to endorse it as cricket books are contracted through only one publisher and have to be a special size. We received a small order from South Africa and after lengthy negotiations sold over 700 to India, however true to rumour they still owe us money. Other countries in both Europe and America bought several copies. The web of Amazon.com was very successful in gaining orders. The Lords' shop was the best seller for cricket ground out sales.

Several cricket retailers took books in bulk to add to their product sales. Some orders were gained through Waterstones and W.H.Smith.

Following the success of Think-Cricket, the next title we launched was PLAN Cricket, which was published by ourselves – Potwell Press in 2003, One of the readers of *THINK-Cricket*, the Chairman of Kerr McGee Oil, Frank Sharratt a keen follower of the game, agreed to sponsor the book. It explained the many requirements of how to run a successful cricket club. The book to date has sold over 1000 copies.

In 1973 when our man joined *The Cricketer*, it was a small team – Ben Brocklehurst, Harry Constantine, Christopher Martin-Jenkins and E.W. 'Jim' Swanton and our man became Advertisement Manager.

In those early days the title had a circulation of 12000 and an advertisement revenue that was slightly less. What the team did have was loads of experience, the will to achieve and knowhow.

Firstly Ben set up offices in his garage and with each of the others working from their own establishments they set about developing the magazine. Ben was Managing Director, was a very good ideas man, Harry was the researcher and linkman with the printer, buying paper, print and costings.

'CM-J' and Jim were the editorial team providing quality written features and articles, their strength was their very strong links with the professionals throughout the world of cricket, coupled with a respect by fellow journalists with whom they asked to contribute to the publication.

Our man steadily built a relationship with potential advertisers and convinced them to spend their promotional budgets within the magazine.

Initially Jackson Rudd & Associates were responsible for

advertisement production but soon handed this mantle to Adpress, headed by John Patrick, including responsibility for Classified Advertisement sales.

The team started slowly, but year by year with hard work they were successful, they created a number of competitions, all were sponsored and every team participating had to have a subscription to the magazine.

Probably the most successful was the National Village knockout, which covered England, Scotland and Wales, of vital interest for the clubs who participated – the final was played at Lord's. Next *The Cricketer* Cup sponsored by Moet & Chandon for 21 years, this was for Old Boy teams of the principle Public Schools – the winning finalist's prize was a day at the Chateau Sarun (Moet's Headquarters) in Rheims with a tour of the Vineyard and the Champagne vaults.

The Colts Trophy for under 15's was a great competition, for it enabled schools from both the Private and Comprehensive sector to compete together. This event was born through the support of The English School's Association – they ran it and it was funded by The Lord's Taverners, the catalyst was Ben Brocklehurst. Hundreds of youngsters from all walks of life were able to play cricket together and the Final was played at Trent Bridge, Nottingham – a Test Match ground.

Other events such as The Company Cup included company teams, the Police and the Civil Service. Whenever a final was played each member of the team carried out the necessary jobs, from selling of tickets, to car parking, looking after guests and making sure the event was a success. For instance, our man ran a 'Throwing the cricket ball competition' prior to the start of the National Village knockout for many years. Over the first twenty years, other sections were added: Cricketer Holidays started with a package to Corfu, this could be most likened to a 'House' party ambiance. Then it was linked to playing cricket in Corfu. Holidays then branched out to a huge range of destinations. Ben's daughter, Charmagne started a magazine shop, this featured 'Mail Order' in the publication and established friends around the world.

The Cricketer International as it became, had several editors during its thirty five odd years in the Brocklehurst reign, somebody who did give a real boost to the circulation was Reg Hayter, Reg supplied young journalists with the knowhow in sports writing, all those with apprenticeships went to work on National newsmedia. A credit to his training. Apart from running his own business he had excellent contacts within cricket and invariably would gain an interview where others had failed.

Our man built the advertisement revenue up from just under £12,000 up to £300,000. In the last few years this averaged out to about £275,000. A large contribution was due to the features he wrote himself, equivalent to sum 40 thousand plus words per annum. The main thrust was a world assessment of cricket equipment, clothing and footwear that was distributed as a supplement with the April issue, at its peak it carried around eighty pages of complimentary advertising and was worth £50,000, this appeared over 28 years – although in its early years it was only a feature article it grew steadily and became very popular as a reader item. Other Features included two features on ground equipment (Spring and Autumn) and a Tours and Touring Supplement with the November issue.

Sadly, due to the equipment feature requirement, it had to be written in January/ February, he had to refuse two separate invitations to write for Air New Zealand on Golden Oldies Festivals – one in Sydney and one in South Africa. Credit should be given to the editorial staff, who in the first place needed to edit his work and their guidance was much appreciated, Peter Perchard was the last Editor and with his team including the assistant Editor Mandy Ripley helped him on many occasions. Mandy, in her spare time spent many hours at Wimbledon Tennis and was reputed to be the unofficial mascot of the British Davis Cup team.

Over a long period firstly as Editor, and then as Editorial Director and often as an advisor Christopher Martin-Jenkins had worked tirelessly for *The Cricketer*, despite his work for *The Daily Telegraph* and latterly the Chief Cricket Correspondent for The *Times*, he was always helpful and provided excellent advice for our man. Many a time he would cut key editorial content to include a late advertisement. But CMJ was also a good friend, an attacking batsman, offbreak bowler and a keen fielder.

But all good things have to end, so when Ben suddenly became ill, his previous direction and careful grooming of those who had helped him build the success of the title, now deserted him and he looked to others for guidance. This marked the beginning of the end. EW 'Jim' Swanton had died and decisions were taken over a few years to undo all the good work the few had achieved in 25 years, the downfall took just over five years.

What went wrong? Of course it is easier in hindsight, but most of the people who had built the title were still available, their pleas were ignored. The title lost their sponsorship and panic set in, again they might have asked those who had set things up in the first place, but no, they decided to sell, but even that had its hurdles and the end was very quick and disastrous to the Few.

It was sad, as at the beginning, Ben had said 'If we make a success of this publication, I will see you are properly rewarded', The Few knew they could trust him, for he was known for his loyalty, but his illness was too great and the forces that followed overtook any decisions he wished to make.

Our man on gaining a new contract telephoned Head

office one afternoon, he was put through to the new Managing Director, who said,

"I have some bad news, You are redundant." When asked from when, the answer was from now, you can finish at the end of the month.

This was after 32 years. He was not invited to attend their offices again.

Once he had recovered from the shock, he approached Hampshire CCC with a proposal of starting a publication for them. However, before the end of the meeting they had invited him to sell ground advertisements for them starting the following week.

Hence 2003 started badly, sales in the new job went well and the ground was full up by the end of May. But the success was short lived, the day-to-day organisation was in turmoil and everyone operated on a knife-edge. On planning for the next season he found one of the professional cricketers had been given winter employment and his services were no longer required. Work was hard to find, he tried various schemes, one was reasonably successful running sales for magnetic wristlets for a company called Ecoflow, but the market became saturated and he moved on to selling for a company who sold advertisements for Doctors' practices on a commission basis, this was intensive and was a stop gap, but he found the publications seldom appeared and he had to drive many miles without adequate reward.

Our man had now reached official retirement age and with another cricket season with time to play and energy levels high he was to have his best ever Hampshire Hogs season taking 74 wickets, this included 39 wickets in nine matches, making him only the second player ever to achieve over sixty wickets in a Hampshire Hogs season and was one behind the record holder Ian Shield for the most wickets in a season. This meant he reached his 100 wickets in a season for the nineteenth time. In First Class cricket Derek Shackleton, another great friend from his early Easter nets, had gained this achievement on 20 occasions.

Another example of how life provides hurdles and it is how you overcome them that matters. All this occurred at the age of 65, indirectly both events would have a lasting effect on his future.

One Autumn day he received a call from a previous competitive magazine called *Cricket World*, they said they respected his various articles on Groundsmanship, Tours & Touring and The Equipment Supplement and asked if he would consider joining them. Demoralised as he was with selling for Doctor Practice booklets, this was a lifeline.

He chose to ignore a warning from a friend, Michael Blumberg, that there might be a hidden agenda.

During his absence from the cricket industry, certain factors had changed, the internet was now in full swing, many of his previous advertisers now had their own websites and magazine advertising budgets had been reduced. But the title for whom he now worked was only published quarterly and did not have the same circulation or impact that he had with *The Cricketer International*. However, they were developing a website of their own and this enabled him to learn this new medium. Communication with the Management was not always straight forward, which did prove a problem for him, for instance he was told the magazine would gain an ABC Certificate in the next two months, but for various reasons over the next eighteen months it never materialised. Sales were hard work, as income was related to either advertisement sales or published editorial, some articles failed to appear and this caused doubt with his clients – The Title's bosses demanded immediate results which could only be built through trust and having gained all his contacts, they said they had decided to handle everything in-house and his services were no longer required. He had been outmanoeuvred, the trust and honour which he believed in was not the ways of this new world. With income at a standstill, radical decisions were required and the family needed to downsize and move and this was achieved. His wife was wonderful throughout standing resolutely beside him and taking the knocks that this new life imposed upon them.

During this period The Bat & Ball Cricket Club was still playing mainly against touring sides. One of these was brought over from Australia by his friend Harry Solomons, his stores based around Sydney also promote youth coaching, cricket tours and also has a large cricket museum. Many leading Australian cricketers started working through Harry's support in the Kingsgrove shop On their tour Harry's team was captained by Doug Walters, one of Australia's legendary batsmen, in their match against The Bat & Ball, our man trapped him caught by Ross Edwards, who represented Australia when Doug Walters was playing in the same side. Ross had retired to England and regularly turned out for the club, he also took part in the Hampshire Hogs Golfing Society days. Another team that visited us was the Drillers CC, run by James Hull, a leading dentist from Harley Street, in London. The team included several of The Glamorgan County cricketers and captained by Matthew Maynard, the match was played in the best competitive manner and The Drillers won off the penultimate ball, a direct throw causing a run out and giving the visitors victory by one run, our man had Matthew stumped off his seventh ball. This featured in a book by Jocelyn Galsworthy called *Lords of Cricket*, in it Matthew stated it as one of his worst moments in cricket.

Probably the most important match for the Club was when they played Hampshire County Cricket Club for the County's Benefit.

One of *The Cricketers*' advertisers was Jocelyn Galsworthy, who has become the leading cricket painter throughout the world, commissioned to paint Test Matches in England, Australia, New Zealand and South Africa.

Her activities have also covered Golf tournaments, Football matches and sporting occasions. She is very well known for her painting of portraits. In 2005 she decided to write her second book, the first had been very successful – *White Hats and Cricket Bats* – in this she had included our man as he had helped her with his range of contacts. In her next book *Lords of Cricket* she painted the portraits of the leading cricketers of the time, the world's Cricket Press and some benefactors of the sport from around the World. Our man was given the great honour of having his portrait included in connection with Broadhalfpenny Down and The Bat & Ball Inn.

He was named 'The Encyclopaedia'.

Only one other person had a building included and he started the book – The Duke of Richmond and Gordon at Goodwood. Our man ended the book.

All the portraits were taken to the House of Lords for the launch. Jocelyn then graciously gave his wife his portrait.

Jocelyn Galsworthy

By Judy Vigors

Have you been to Lord's lately? Do you enter this hallowed ground by the Grace Gates? If you do you will see, directly in front of you, a smart booth with bay trees outside, bearing the legend Jocelyn Galsworthy – Originals and Limited Edition Cricket Prints and overhead, far too big to miss, a poster of the lady herself in a white, floppy hat seated at her easel painting the very ground you have come to see. Thus the original, one-off doyenne of the art of painting cricket matches announces herself today. She has come a long, long way from the somewhat gauche ingénue she once was, via art lessons at the Winchester College of Art, course at studios in Paris, Spain and Germany and the first tentative sales and exhibitions held in friends' houses in London.

Jocelyn has just celebrated 25 years of painting cricket and has achieved a remarkable success by a combination of dedication, determination and natural cussedness which has seen her stick rigidly to her plan to be the foremost cricketing artist in the world. Life has not always been easy for her and she was not born with the proverbial spoon either, but with her mother's help and guidance her own perseverance paid dividends with the result that her portraits, seascapes, landscapes, golfing and cricket paintings are now much sought after. Nor is painting the extent of her talents. Jocelyn is one of the world's great givers – she gives of her time to causes in which she believes or which touch her heart in some way and her friends can always rely on her generosity when it comes to raising money for good causes. She has donated paintings on many occasions to raise money for charitable purposes, especially for cricket for the disabled or disadvantaged. She is a Trustee of the Arundel Foundation which aims to provide time away in the beautiful Sussex countryside at Arundel for disadvantaged and difficult children from the inner cities. There they can practice in the marvellous indoor school funded by Paul Getty, play cricket on Arundel's beautiful ground and be influenced for good by Johnny Barclay and others who dedicate their time to the project. Honorary membership of the Lady Taverners continues the charitable theme and Jocelyn is also an Associate Member of MCC, a longstanding Member of Hampshire CCC and generally welcome at any cricket club whether at home or abroad.

Travelling abroad with Jocelyn, on painting expeditions to cricketing countries such as Australia, South Africa and New Zealand is a never-to-be forgotten experience. I shall certainly never forget our time together in Australia. Air travel had to be business class at worst and first class if possible. That put a permanent hole in the finances before we even started! With the amount of paraphernalia an artist has to carry, including easel, canvasses, paints and sundry equipment, we looked like a travelling circus and when one is as particular as Jocelyn, cries of "Don't drop my easel!" and "*Do* be careful with that!" or "Haven't you seen a box of paints before?" (this to Customs at Adelaide) or "I don't care if my easel *is* made of wood, you are not going to confiscate it!" can bring on a sudden headache and a feeling that one would rather be elsewhere. Checking into the hotel can be a bit of an ordeal. Everything has to be immaculate. Fortunately for Australia everything was, especially the fantastic Adelaide Oval. Having lunch there in the Don Bradman Room was a special treat and Jocelyn loved it. She is now so well-known that people come up to her in all situations and want to talk cricket. Sometimes they have seen her on the television and acknowledge her as a "celebrity". Unlike the tinsel and plastic celebrities of today,

Jocelyn never puts on a public face. What you see is what you get at all times. She is exactly the same at home on the Isle of Wight as at a big dinner at Lord's. If you step out of line, she will let you know.

There does not seem much left for Jocelyn to achieve, but she is not aware of the fact. Her diary is full for the year and it never occurs to her that it would be good to take a break. Holidays, clearly, are for wimps. When she is not travelling round the British Isles completing commissions, she is hard at work in her Studio on the Isle of Wight, paintbrushes in one hand and telephone in the other, putting the finishing touches to portraits or cricket scenes or charming colour-washed pen and ink sketches of life at Lord's during the Season. She has depicted the Jazz Band, the Harris Garden, the Members' dash through the Grace Gates on the morning of the first Ashes Test and countless dramatic oil paintings of the ground itself, before and after the Media Centre and the repositioning of Old Father Time. The Test Match Special team invariably gives her a mention and the camera homes in on her latest creation, dwelling for several seconds on the floppy white hat which has become Jocelyn's trademark. They never catch her out – she is always at her easel, paintbrush poised. At suitable intervals, the artist visits her 'shop' to greet the public, some of whom will buy her limited edition prints. There are many to choose from. Some of her original work is also on display and sales for these expensive items are not slow, either.

Jocelyn has, also, published two books. Her first, 'White Hats and Cricket Bats' is an autobiography and an interesting account of her early life, her somewhat unconventional upbringing and her overwhelming desire to succeed at her chosen profession. The book is filled with her early work, mostly portraits and the beginnings of her love of cricket and her depiction of the game using pastels rather than oils. She has now largely abandoned pastels as they are tricky to use when painting outside.

Her second book, bears the name 'Lords of Cricket' and contains some marvellous drawings of present and past cricketers, not playing and not in their whites, but head and shoulder portraits as they look today. Captains of England Michael Vaughan, Andrew Strauss and Andrew Flintoff as well as Captain of Australia, Ricky Ponting are some of the distinguished players of yesteryear. Umpires Dickie Bird and the late Shep feature as do Administrators, the Test Match Special Team (including the late Bill Frindall) and other, perhaps unsung, heroes.

I have not heard via the grapevine or anywhere else that Jocelyn is planning a third book. But it would not surprise me in the least. Jocelyn's output is prolific, her talent undisputed and her ambition as keen as ever. What next? By way of relaxation, Jocelyn might do a series of beautiful village grounds. She could wander from place to place, staying at charming country inns (with first-class restaurants), painting this quintessentially English game, making suggestions to surprised villagers on how to improve their facilities.... They might be forgiven for thinking that Dame Margaret Rutherford had come to call.

Doug Walters

by Ross Edwards

At first sight, Doug Walters was the archetypal Australian hero, a boy from the bush, wiry, hard, laconic in speech and action but with a cricketing attitude everyone loved…. If the ball is there, hit it. It wasn't his technique that was attractive so much as his attacking attitude which said to the bowlers… "I'm coming to get you if you don't get me!"

Square of the wicket shots were played with fearless aggression and he had a unique "coming to attention" back foot drive. During the early 1970s, if anyone was asked whom they would pick first in the Australian side, most would nominate 'Freddie'.

'Freddie' was his nickname, (universally used by his team mates) given to him during a South African tour as one of "the dunce brothers, Herbie, Bertie and Freddie".

There have been many good Test batsmen, but only very few are capable of changing the course of a Test.. He was truly one.

In the first Ashes Test against England in Brisbane in 1974 after the first innings there was little between the sides and the match was evenly balanced. Then Australia lost three or four early wickets so that the balance swung firmly in England's favour. Doug came in with Australia in trouble facing a battery of England fast bowlers who had bounced him out in the first innings.It was only a question of whether he was going to get a bouncer first or second ball.

It was second ball and it disappeared through a beautiful hook well in front of square leg. The next ball was similarly pulled viciously just wide of mid on. Two incredible shots in the context of the match and his experience in the first innings.

He went on the attack and played a brilliant innings which changed the momentum of the match. England were then finished off by the pace and hostility of Dennis Lillee and Jeff Thomson.

In the following Test played on the hard, fast WACA pitch, he came in to bat just before tea and at the break was three not out. In the last session he played a wonderful array of strokes to be 90 odd not out at the commencement of the final over.

It was no secret that he was going to be attacked with short pitched bowling. He hooked at and missed two of them. From another hook he got a top edge for four and with the final ball he middled a hook off Bob Willis that sailed flat and sweetly in front of square for six to bring up his century and 100 runs in the session.

He has scored 100 runs in a session on three occasions. Once in New Zealand, another time in Guyana when he also opened the bowling, and that memorable time in Perth.

He is also a joker and regularly played all manner of tricks on team mates. One time during a Test in Melbourne he took a plastic spider onto the field and stuck it to the ball with chewing gum while fielding at 3rd slip before throwing the ball (with spider) to the gully fieldsman who was terrified of all types of creepy crawlies. On catching the ball, gully nearly had a heart attack much to the amusement of the rest of the team.

Doug had surprising speed in the field, being one of the best but largely unrecognised cover fieldsmen. I recall early in my first tour to England fielding in the covers and looking around found I was between Greg Chappell and Doug Walters. I vividly recall thinking "It doesn't get any better than this!"

He earned a reputation when bowling as a partnership breaker. While this was true as he took many wickets when they were most needed, he was always a danger when he came on to bowl. He commanded a deceptive amount of swing allied to consistent length.

Always thinking he had a range of balls, some of which were 'the running in faster slower ball', 'the running in slower faster ball', 'the running in faster faster ball', and to complete the package, 'the running in slower slower ball'. Many batsmen fell to his cunning variation should they relax momentarily or fail to treat his apparent innocuous deliveries with utmost respect.

Always good company, he is a formidable card player as he 'remembers' cards. In Lismore (in north western New South Wales) the NSW team arrived to play a Sheffield Shield match. It was late in the evening and we all repaired to the only establishment open which was the local RSL Club. There was no one else around when a large group of menacing bikers arrived and settled themselves at the other end of the bar.

There was tension in the air, but Freddie (who was everyone's hero) walked over to them, introduced himself and bought them a beer. So we spent a pleasant evening. He smoked continuously and drank steadily for extended periods. Lately, he has given up cigarettes, something his past team mates cannot believe.

There is no doubt that after Freddie was made, they broke the mould.

Ross Edwards

By Ross Edwards

When I first played at Warnford, I was batting when Christopher Bazalgette came on to bowl. I had known him previously, but not on the cricket field. As is my wont, I treated his first over with considerable respect, being mindful of his reputation.

I watched closely for devious machinations, skilful variation of flight or formidable spin, all of which could have earned him such a wicket taking reputation. Finding none, I proceeded to commit suicide by trying to slog him over the deep midwicket boundary and only succeeded in holing out to a cunningly placed deep fieldsman.

I am one of many hundreds of batsmen, good, bad, smart and dumb, who have fallen to a man who knows what he bowls, spins a web for the batsman and knows how to set a field for his bowling.

The road to capitulation at the hands of the "Gette" was long and eventful. In my early '20s I played Grade cricket in Perth as a wicket keeper, following in the footsteps of my father, who represented Western Australia. I had moderate success with the bat and was included in the WA state squad and in 1964 played in my first Sheffield Shield match.

I didn't play the following year but then our wicket-keeper was selected in the Australian team to tour South Africa. Hence I became my state's 'keeper. I made some runs but didn't distinguish myself too well with the gloves and realised I had no future behind the stumps.

When our wicket-keeper returned the following season, I was included as a batsman and found myself in the field for the first time. As an international hockey player, I was fast over 20 yards and could turn at speed which made me an ideal cover point fieldsman.

I was not a pretty or graceful fieldsman, falling over (which was often mistaken for diving) in order to prevent the ball getting past, but it was very effective in terms of keeping a batsman on strike. Thus it was through my Test career.

I scored sufficient runs to continue to be selected as a batsman and developed slowly, gradually moving up the order to Number four, where I batted for most of my first-class career. From 1964 to 1975 I scored 14 centuries and was part of a very successful Western Australian team, firstly under the captaincy of Tony Lock and then John Inverarity. In 1971-72 I had a particularly good year, scoring four centuries, and Western Australia won the Sheffield Shield.

When Australia's team to tour England in 1972 was selected, there were six Western Australians, including me. As an Australian cricketer this is a crowning moment. But I was already 30 years old with a job, a family and little likelihood of more than a brief Test career, so I resolved to give 100 per cent in effort every time.

While I was mature in years and worldly experience (as an qualified accountant) I was a babe in terms of international cricket experience. I cannot tell you how proud I was to step onto the field wearing the "baggy green" cap. My first tour of England (which incidentally is the most desirable tour of all) was highly enjoyable.

Under our captain, Ian Chappell, we played the game the right way, attacking when at all possible and defending only when there was no alternative. We set out to score as many runs as fast as possible in the first innings so as to give our attack (Lillee, Massie, Colley, Mallett) time to get the opposition out. Ian's field placings were always positive and many times I found myself very lonely at cover point as most fielders were behind the stumps.

Ian was a great leader of good players. He believed in them, expecting them to be the best at their particular talent and always to give of their best. So he gave everyone freedom to express that talent. It was a joy to play under him.

The first Test of that series was at Old Trafford, which we lost. I was 12th man. My first appearance was at Lord's. What an occasion, for it was also Bob Massie's first Test. He took eight wickets in each innings, which devastated England and squared the series. I batted once, making 28.

I can't remember much about this innings, as Lord's is pretty overwhelming, particularly to overseas players. A special victory in my first Test, a visit to Buckingham Palace to meet the Queen, and a member of the Australian cricket team.....it doesn't get any better.

Then to Trent Bridge for the 3rd Test. Batting at number five, I scored a paltry 12 in the first innings. One of our openers suffered a migraine and was unable to bat in the second innings. I suggested to the captain that I should open the innings as a stand-in opener rather than dropping everyone down the order and disrupting their normal positions. It wasn't that I was particularly confident of making runs - in fact I wasn't.

At the time, he dismissed the suggestion with a few non-repeatable well chosen words, but as we walked off the field he told me to put my pads on. I opened with Keith Stackpole, who had scored a century in the first innings, so naturally the thrust of the attack was directed towards him.

He got out and Ian Chappell came in, so naturally he was the focus of the bowler's attention. He, too, was dismissed and Greg Chappell came in to bat following his imperious century at Lord's.

At stumps we were still both in. I had made 90 and no-one had noticed!

On the Monday after the rest day (which we used to have on Sundays in that era) I proceeded quietly to my maiden Test century, which, incidentally, was the first ever by a Western Australian, something of which I am particularly proud. At this stage England went completely to pieces in both bowling and fielding and we scored at will until the declaration, at which time I remained not out with 170 to my name.

The pitch was so true we were unable to dismiss England and the match terminated in an unsatisfactory draw. In the next Test at Headingley, the selectors picked me to open the innings on the basis of my batting at Trent Bridge, despite my suggesting that this was not a good idea. I was proved right as I was out in both innings without scoring. This was the "fusarium wicket". . . Enough said.

This tour, while not successful in terms of winning back the Ashes, was a turning point in Australia's cricket fortunes. Back home, we played a series against Pakistan which we won 3-0. The third Test in Sydney provided one of the most improbable results, for we came back from an impossible situation to win. In the final innings I took what has to rank as one of the best outfield catches in Test history (a modest but accurate comment).

I played in only two of these Tests, scoring runs in both, and was selected in the team to tour West Indies in 1973. Apart from my batting, I was chosen as the second wicket keeper and as Rod Marsh had every second match off, I played in all the Island matches as well as the Tests.

I scored runs in the first Test but was a disappointment after that. I didn't realise until much later that I was physically exhausted and kept getting out in the '20s through loss of concentration. This series was memorable for the outstanding win we had against the odds in the third Test In Trinidad.

I found I was omitted from the next Australia tour, which was to New Zealand. While disappointed, I was probably lucky as I doubt I would have had the skill to play on their slow, low pitches. The next season, I resolved to give my best to see if I could regain my place in the team as England were touring in 1974-75.

If I did not achieve that, then I would still have had had a highly memorable time and I would still be Australian cricketer number 289. I scored runs in the early Shield matches and was selected for the first Test in Brisbane. This was highly memorable as it was when Jeff Thomson was first released onto the unsuspecting English batsmen. No-one who was not there can comprehend how fast and dangerous he really was.

I scored a couple of half centuries and continued in the side for the second Test in Perth. Here Lillee and Thomson again dominated despite the extremely gallant efforts of Colin Cowdrey.

Australia were thrilled by Doug Walters' century in the final session, culminating with a flat six off the last ball of the day. I batted through the session with him and accumulated 80, finishing 90 not out at stumps. Next morning I was on strike and ran five twos to bring up my century. But in doing so, I wore Doug out so that he hung his bat out at the first ball he faced and was out without addition to his score.

It is hard to explain how extremely dangerous Lillee and Thomson (particularly Thomson) were in this series - much more so than they were in England in subsequent encounters. I was extremely glad to be on the Australian side.

Shortly after this series ended with Australia winning back the Ashes, the team to compete in the first World Cup in England was selected. Joy of joys, I was again included. We reached the final only to be beaten by West Indies after the longest day's cricket in history. I contributed to our defeat by dropping Clive Lloyd at square leg when he was on about ten, thus allowing the world to see one of the truly great one day innings,

I also dropped Rohan Kanhai at deep square leg before he scored.

So I was 150 down before we batted!

Following this experimental World Cup, Australia stayed on in England for a four Test series. The first was at Edgbaston. England won the toss and put us in, relying on what turned out to be an erroneous weather forecast. We accumulated a score of 350 against some outstanding bowling, particularly by John Snow, who while past his best, was still formidable. The luck just ran our way. We caught England on a wet pitch twice, and that was the end of Mike Denness as their captain.

The next Test was at Lord's. We lost wickets very quickly so I went in to bat at an early stage. The pitch was good, the outfield fast and the bowlers bowled to my one strength, the square cut. When they pitched it up, the ball was on leg stump. Cricket doesn't get any easier than this!

The impending century was not a matter of concern. All I had to do was stay in and it was a given. The circumstances were so propitious that 200 looked like a real possibility. I'd never scored a double century before and there was no better time than now.

It was an innocuous medium paced ball bowled by Bob Woolmer, a delivery of no account. I just planned to push it wide of mid on, take the single, confirm 100 and proceed to 200. But I missed it. Out plumb lbw for 99.

Batting that day must have been easy, for Dennis Lillee made 70. In the second innings, England again had us on the run and I found myself batting with Greg Chappell to save the match. This we did, and my unbeaten half century in this innings was a better achievement than my first innings batting.

The next Test at Headingley was shaping to be one of the great contests as we were chasing more than 300 in the last innings and reckoned we could get them. Then some politically motivated vandals dug up the wicket.

The final Test at the Oval was a damp squib as it was played on the flattest pitch ever seen. It was impossible to dismiss a side twice and so my final Test finished in a forgettable draw. Following retirement from first-class cricket, I took on the job of captaining and coaching a local grade side in Perth. We were beaten in the final the first year and won in the second year.

Then came Kerry Packer's World Series Cricket. This was without doubt the highest standard of cricket ever played. I was mainly in the reserve squad for the 2 years. During this period I had moved to Sydney and in due course I played for New South Wales for one season and captained my local grade club.

I retired in 1981 and didn't play again until I moved to London in 1994. Then I went down to my local club in Shepherds Bush and practised and played with their 3rd X1. I loved it. After three years I was transferred to Singapore for five years and played for my local club.

On my return to England, I once again joined a local Club, Byfleet, where I played in their second team for four seasons. I also played with a variety of teams: Lord's Taverners, Forty Club, Hampshire Hogs, Flemish Giants, MCC and many more, playing at such memorable grounds as Warnford, Broadhalfpenny Down at Hambledon, Ashford and others whose names are a blur but are still vivid in my memory.

CHAPTER 7

The Benefit

The milk of Human kindness – wonderful friends…

In 2006, Christopher decided he should not apply to play in Hogs' fixtures as this might mean a younger player would be omitted. So he advised the club that he would be available but that he could only be picked in the week prior to any fixture taking place. He would ensure a team would not be a man short.

The Hogs had given our man 40 years of wonderful pleasure and he knew he had many friends of all age groups. This famous club has done so much for him, both on and off the field. But to his surprise and joy they now surpassed all that had gone before. They offered him a Benefit Dinner, which would take place at the Rose Bowl, Hampshire's ground, in September 2007. They would help him create a Benefit brochure and arrange prizes for an auction. Peter Came, Rupert Cox and Jonathan Grant, agreed to plan and arrange the event.

Christopher asked leading writers to provide copy for the brochure. Peter Dunn compiled it and helped with the layout and did the statistics. Came orchestrated the fundraising and all three gave up huge amounts of their time.

The invitation is printed below, followed by the Benefit Brochure. Jocelyn Galsworthy very generously donated an original painting and a special print to the auction and many friends supported the dinner. At the beginning of the evening they displayed the video in which Christopher had interviewed Ali G. Robin Smith, the former Hampshire captain, who had written the foreword in Christopher's book *Think-Cricket*, kindly spoke on the night of his own birthday and was one of the last to leave, a huge compliment to our man. A fund-raising Benefit is virtually unknown for amateur cricketers and this financial support threw him a lifeline when work problems were at their worst.

The Christopher Bazalgette

Retirement and Benefit Dinner

Thursday 13th September 2007

THE ROSE BOWL

The Rose Bowl
The Hampshire Suite

7.00 pm for 7.30 pm

Guest Speaker: Robin Smith (Hampshire and England)
Master of Ceremonies: Shaun Udal (Hampshire and England)

Cost: £65 or £600 for a Table of 10

RSVP
The Christopher Bazalgette Retirement and Benefit Dinner
c/o Jonathan Grant,
Laverstoke Grange, Laverstoke, Whitchurch,
Hampshire, RG28 7PF

I would like to book .... tickets for the Bazalgette Dinner
I would like to join.................'s table

I would like to reserve a table for 10 ☐ Yes ☐ No

Or

I would like to make a donation
of ....to the Bazalgette
Retirement Fund

I enclose my cheque for £............. made
payable to the Christopher Bazalgette
Retirement and Benefit Dinner

CHRISTOPHER BAZALGETTE BENEFIT BROCHURE

A Personal Message (from Christopher Bazalgette)
'When I joined the Hampshire Hogs in 1966, I was working for the late Ben Brocklehurst and one of my clients was Engelmann & Buckham. So it was decided that the late Arthur Buckham should propose and Ben would second me. I came to the club as an opening batsman.

My association with the County Club is much longer, when aged 11 – 13. I had 'Lofty' Herman as my Prep. School coach and Easter nets with Johnny Arnold, Arthur Holt, Desmond Eagar and Jimmy Gray. In those 'heady' days I also operated the scoreboards at Northlands Road and Bournemouth, often travelling on the team bus. Later I met Nigel Robson, Christopher Van der Noot, Andrew Benke and George Bowyer.

After four years of batting for the Hogs, I found I still had the ability to swing the ball even though I now bowled slow to very slow. I decided to develop this unusual style. I am indebted to many Hogs, club officers, captains, wicket-keepers and fielders for their athletism and help in capturing victims!

I have an apology for Bill Hughes and his various groundsmen to whom I cajoled in my keenness to play in adverse conditions.

I would like to thank all the writers and advertisers for their wonderful support of this Benefit brochure. Finally, June and I would like to thank Prontaprint, Richard Sanger and Peter Dunn for their expertise in compiling this brochure and to Judy Harrison for allowing me to include the picture of Broadhalfpenny Down on the cover.

A leader from Rupert Cox
Former Hampshire County cricketer

There are few cricketers who are still playing at nigh on 69, but Christopher David Evelyn Bazalgette is no ordinary cricketer. His Hampshire Hog tally in excess of 1300 wickets makes him an exceptional protagonist of that artful practice of flight, guile and deception. But for a persistent knee problem, forcing him down the batting order, 'Gette' would surely be a Hog rival to Wilfred Rhodes.

Rhodes claimed an astonishing 4187 first-class victims, and added 39,802 runs for good measure.

If you consider that Rhodes played day in, day out and that the Gette has taken plenty of non-Hog wickets as well, it further illustrates his achievements.

Out of interest I thumbed through my Wisden Almanac to view the first-class players who have similar number of career wickets: Mushtaq Ahmed, Shane Warne and Muttiah Muralitharan!

There is, of course, more to the 'Gette' than mere statistics. He has been a fine team man and Hog man through and through. Many a Hog will have leant heavily on Christopher for support, when at the eleventh hour their team sheet for the weekend is decidedly threadbare. As we all know, he always delivered.

I, for one, count myself very fortunate to have played alongside 'Gette'. The day that Hampshire CCC decided I was too immature to continue on their playing staff, he was straight on the phone asking how he could help. And, when another poor shot has cost my wicket and I'm sitting in the dressing-room, pint in hand, contemplating golf or a dirty weekend, there he is to pacify the mind and cleanse the soul. He has been a fine servant to the Hampshire Hogs and we owe him plenty.

Bazalgette will never retire, he will bowl less maidens over!

Gette Stat Attack!
Stand by for the vital statistics automatically updated every time the Gette plays – Daily!

Christopher's Hog bowling figures defy belief – a miserly average of 20.36 with a sensational strike rate of 34.00. His total wicket haul of 1404 almost doubles that of Francis Irving, the next man on the aggregate list!

Hampshire Hogs
Number of seasons   44

Bowling:	Overs	Maidens	Runs	Wickets	Average
	7569	979	27191	1335	20.36

Batting:	Played	Innings	Not Out	Total Runs	Average
	771	347	159	2042	10.86

Average: 20.73   Strike Rate: 34   Run rate 3.76

Best Bowling
39 wickets in 9 consecutive matches aged 65.
Gained 4 or more wickets in an innings on 93 occasions.

Overall
- Gained a total of 3824 wickets
- Achieved a 100 wickets in a season 19 times.
- Best analysis – 2 for 36
- Playing for India Gymkhana v The full Indian Test team (1983)
-5 for 76 Hampshire Hogs v. Hampshire CCC

Test Cricketer scalps
- Henk Moll (Holland);
- Doug Walters, Ross Edwards (Australia);
- Kirti Azad, Ravi Sasri (India);
- John Starling, Jeff Crowe (New Zealand);
- Kevan James, Matthew Maynard, Chris Smith, John
        Stephenson, Paul Terry (England)

Overall Best Analysis
 9 for 20 Hambledon v Emsworth

Broadhalfpenny Brigands Amateur record
8 for 79 for Broadhalfpenny Brigands v London New Zealand

A little persuasion has elicited figures for all his cricket since school and his total wicket haul stands at a monumental 3824!! This places him handily at No 2 if this figure is inserted into the all time first class list:

W.Rhodes	4187
CDE Bazalgette	**3824**
AP Freeman	3776

Note: These figures have been updated to include every year to the end of 2010.

* * * * *

Article by Christopher D.A. Martin-Jenkins former Editorial Director of The Cricketer International, *Chief Cricket Correspondent for The* Times *and 2011 President of the Marylebone Cricket Club, and long standing member of the Test Match Special team.*

Christopher Bazalgette took over the business of selling advertisements for *The Cricketer* soon after the late Ben Brocklehurst had bought the magazine from its former disinterested managers in 1972. Another keen club cricketer, Colin Pegley of Amersham Cricket Club, had done the job until then, but he had other masters to serve and fewer contacts in the game than the thick set, red-headed, slightly Evelyn Waughish character who now set about the difficult business of selling space in a periodical which at that stage had quite a small circulation.

Chris played a big part in the rise in circulation and the considerable rise in profits that followed. He knew his business inside out, had a host of friends in the game and a gently persuasive way about him. That determined jut in the jaw was not only seen at its most effective when he had just been struck for three sixes over the nearest hedge (all part of the bowler's cunning plan, of course) or when the Hogs were in a bit of trouble and some stubborn left-handed stone-walling was called for: it came in handy too when he was having a salad lunch in the pavilion with the commercial manager of BMW who had no idea when he sat next to the chap who has just had him caught in the deep for 48 that he would soon be ordering six full page advertisements.

From my point of view Chris could sometimes be a damned nuisance. He talked me into a big feature on new cricket equipment every Spring which soon became a special supplement to the magazine and provided a valuable service to, for example, groundsmen wondering what mower to order or parents which bat to choose for their suddenly hooked seven year old sons.

I knew, of course, that advertisements were crucial to *The Cricketer*'s viability but occasionally one would have some attractive double page feature prepared on some promising young cricketer Graeme Hick, shall we say, of whom very few had heard at the time-only for the phone to ring a couple of days before that month's issue went to press.

'Christopher? It's Christopher Bazalgette here. You're not going to thank me for this. I've got a late ad from Gray-Nicolls. Full colour. That puts me up to 21 pages. Not bad really. In fact it's a record but we won't worry about that now. The thing is, it has to be on a centre page and in full colour.'

"But that's where we have put the feature on young Graeme Hick'.

"Can't you put it somewhere else?"

"No. All other space is catered for."

"It is very important that we keep Gray-Nicolls on side. They have promised me several more if we give this one a good show."

"Oh, alright then. I'll cut Hick to one page."

"You're a trooper, Sir: Now to more important things. Did I tell you what happened when I came on at Warnford last week when the Foresters were 94 for no wicket ten minutes before tea?"

There was no arguing with C.B. It was all done with such courtesy, if necessary with a bit of flattery too, and with an audible smile on the telephone or a visual one in person. He has always had an enthusiasm that cannot be dimmed and even if he never persuaded you to put an ad in *The Cricketer*, you are in a small club if you never holed out to him.

* * * * *

Article by Robert Kitson who is Rugby Union Correspondent of The Guardian.

It was the same in county cricket in the 1970s and 1980s. Visiting players would barely have parked their cars before rushing to the pavilion to check the home team sheet. Winning the toss at Hampshire and choosing to bat, for example, was a whole different ball game if Andy Roberts or Malcolm Marshall were playing. It has been the same at Warnford for years.

Hush, hush, hush, here comes the bogeyman. Don't let him come too close to you, he'll catch you if he can.

Or, to be precise, have you caught somewhere in a Venus flytrap of his own deliberate creation. No-one has ever placed a field with more care than Christopher Bazalgette, nor snared so many victims who never thought it would happen to them. If you see a middle-aged cricketer with his head clutched in both hands, moaning softly and threatening to give up the game immediately, the chances are he's just lobbed one of the Gette's grenades to wide mid-off.

Having had the privilege of keeping wicket to the great man for the past 25 years, I can also say that no player in my experience has ever approached the crease looking less like a bowler about to take four for 46. On windy days, tottering in, it felt as if you were watching something on the seabed straining against a strong current, its tentacles hanging on by a thread. Newcomers to Warnford would giggle and lick their lips. They seldom made double figures.

The mere statistics, of course, do not provide the full picture. There may never have been a cricketer who has consistently played through more pain for so many decades, moved with the grace of an arthritic stork in the covers or spent more hours modelling the garishly-striped Hog blazer. He has written more books on cricket than some so-called gurus of the game and invented everything from revolutionary sightscreens to slip-catching machines, some of which people even bought. I have seen him angry, irritated, cross, sore, inebriated and ecstatic but never once have I ever known him anything less than 100 per cent obsessed by the game of cricket.

In fact, if there is a first class player to whom he bears a resemblance it is probably Geoffrey Boycott. In Sir Geoffrey's case it was the endless pursuit of 'roons' which drove him and the Gette's hunger for wickets has been equally single-minded. Imagine Chris with a Barnsley accent and the similarity is almost uncanny. 'Young man, that was a terrible shot'. Both of them had a penchant for bowling with their caps on and, while the Gette's batting average is slightly less impressive, he can probably claim a comparable strike rate.

Even Boycs, mind you, has never been on national television teaching Borat how to play the forward defensive shot. If you have never seen the clip, it is out there on the web somewhere and is utterly priceless. But, make no mistake, so is Gette. It is only when you pass the age of 40 yourself that you fully appreciate the monumental stamina, desire and sheer bloody-mindedness he must posess. He grew up in an age before isotonic drinks and gym sessions yet still plays more games per season than men half his age.

My abiding memory when he does finally limp away will be the gentle away floater, artfully disguised, which accounted for so many of his wickets. He was lucky, in some ways, to play so much cricket before heavy bats became so prevalent, let alone the reverse sweep, On the rare occasions he took sustained heavy punishment it was usually on hot, dry days to powerful batsmen with a good eye who swept him over mid-wicket blithely unaware of his reputation. Those who knew him generally played with far less freedom. The sheer horror of getting out to the Gette turned even the best players into quivering wrecks.

Hopefully, there will be a few more wickets to come. It will be a much duller game without him and the Hogs will be hard-pressed to find another bowler who comes halfway to matching his achievements or employing the same field placings. I've always loved the story, true or not of his 50th birthday cake. Apparently 49 of the candles were on the off-side. Well played Gette, and apologies again for all those missed stumpings.

The Christopher Bazalgette Benefit Dinner

Auction

Bottle of Domaine Leroy Vosne-Romanee 1995
1 er Cru Les Chaumesy
Kindly donated by Bob Harding

Set of 8 prints by Rob Perry
Kindly donated by Nick Syrett

"The Spirit of Cricket"
Kindly donated by the artist Jocelyn Galsworthy.
A print of Shane Warne and Kevin Pietersen, Ashes 2005
Signed and Numbered by the artist
Also signed by the two players
Jocelyn Galsworthy has been painting professionally for
over forty years and is particularly well known for her
portraiture and her highly acclaimed paintings of
English and International cricket scenes.

Great niece of the distinguished novelist and playwright
John Galsworthy OM, Jocelyn comes from an artistically
talented family. She has gained an enviable reputation as an
outstanding cricketing artist and has travelled the world
painting Test Matches as well as County, Village, school and
club grounds. The woman in the white hat, sitting on the
boundary, recording matches for posterity, has now become
a part of the world cricket scene.

Hampshire v Sussex Hove 2006
Original Painting donated by Jocelyn Galsworthy

This delightful oil on canvas painting shows
Mushtaq Ahmed bowling to Shane Warne with Nick
Pothas at the non-striker's end.
(Unframed, 18" x 36")

A Signed Bat

From the
1980 Ashes England v Australia Centenary Match at Lords
kindly donated by Alan Burridge

Finally, following a visit to Christopher's loft

A lavishly signed bat from the 1979 International Batsman
of the Year Festival organised by Christopher at The Oval.
Features leading players worldwide:
Proctor, Barry Richards, Hadlee, Lloyd, David Gower etc.

Programme for the Evening

Timings may be wayward, like the occasional Gette
delivery!

7.00 for 7.30 pm	Hampshire Suite, Rose Bowl
	M.C. Rupert Udal
8. 00 pm	Dinner
9.00 pm	Spoof Heads & Tails Jonathan Grant
9.30 pm	Auction after Dessert
10.00 pm	Robin Smith Christopher Bazalgette
11.30 pm	Carriages

Star Guest

Robin Smith, our guest speaker is 44 and 0 days old today – in other word's it's his birthday! Congratulations.

It does not seem that long ago that we all felt sorry for that man on the square cover boundary as Robin's eyes lit up at the sight of a short one about to be given the square cut treatment!

This and other trade mark shots in 62 Tests brought him 4236 runs, 9 hundreds and an average of 45.65, a figure that places him 26th on England's 'all-time' list.

West Indian 'chin music' was even enjoyed at times and we all wondered why England released him while his average was higher than any contemporary England player at the time.

These days (2007) Robin fronts 'Judges Tours' travelling the cricket playing world with 11 tours to date following England's fortunes. Next March it's New Zealand. Judges Tours can be contacted on 07768 553636.

A big thank you for supporting this event.

*   *   *   *   *

The Man Who Took the Pace off the Ball

Chris Bazalgette who first joined the Forty Club in 1077, is renowned for inventing the art of taking the pace off the ball. It's a phrase whch is now commonplace, especially at televised one day cricket. Coaches are always extolling the virtues of pace reduction but it took them a lot of time before they adopted the Bazalgette method. Too long in my view.

Like one of his ancestors – the man who introduced the idea of building sewers under the streets of London – Chris has pioneered features of the great game, including the uncapped knee as opposed to the normal kneecap. The almost total elimination of the run up and static fielding.

Last year he announced his retirement but John Widgery, the superfit Fixture's Secretary of the Forty Club told me: 'I played with him recently and he was up to his usual tricks. There was a strong side wind, left to right, and when he bowled at that end, he proceeded to drift the ball against the wind. Some balls went the way the batsman expected coming in from the off but it was disconcerting. And the pace of the ball got slower and slower'.

Instead of penalty bowl outs, cricket should stage slow lob contests. Who is the bowler who takes most pace off the ball? Chris would be one of the favourites but my money is on Tony MacDonald-Barker; who is still wheeling high into the stratosphere and taking wickets.

Chris was one of the last cricketers to address a misdirected delivery from a bowler which came to rest. He said 'I was playing against Portsmouth Grammar School (pre-David Cameron) and only the umpires and I knew the Law which then required no-one to move with the exception of the batsman. I proceeded to show the boys how to do it. I then hit the ball for four. This Law has now changed – the ball is now deemed 'dead'.

One of his most memorable matches for the XL was against the Paul Getty XI when he was made 12th man. 'We were bowled out for 120 by a young side of County cricketers and when the XL fielded the first change bowler twisted both ankles delivering his first ball, hence I had to go on'.

Thankfully, I had little to do but I had played at Wormsley. Met and chatted with Sir Paul Getty and I thoroughly enjoyed the occasion'.

Seriously, CDEB has put a tremendous amount of enthusiasm back into the game and the Forty Club is in his debt. He served fourteen years on the Executive Committee; nine years as South District Chairman, three years as Marketing Committee chairman and five years as Cricket

Committee Chairman, He wrote the first Newsletter and also created the Inter District Knockout Tournament and in 2006 was made an Honorary Fellow – a good fellow!

I wish him well.

Written by Brian Scovell of the Daily Mail
Author of Brian Lara, cricket's troubled genius.

* * * * *

As well as being a Life member of the Hampshire Hogs Christopher is associated with numerous cricket clubs:

Honorary Fellow of The Forty Club

A member of MCC (over 30 years)

Overseas member for Auckland Cricket Society (NZ)

Overseas Hon. Life member for The Willows CC (NZ)

Overseas Hon. Life member for Crusaders CC (Aus)

Chairman Life President/Co-Founder of The Bat & Ball
    CC

Hon. Life member of Hambledon CC

* * * * *

You only need to see Christopher bowl an over of what might be called 'bazaldrops' to know he is a crafty old thing. He has learnt from long experience that spin is but an accessory, and that line and length, coupled with even the gentlest of parabolas, will lure batsmen of every sort and kind to their doom. I am sure many an over of his must have read ..4.6W

So it was no surprise to find, on one's arrival in Antigua in April 1995, that he had landed himself a nice little winter job, acting as liaison officer between Sandals and the cricket writers covering the Australian tour of the Caribbean.

Renowned for their all-inclusive holiday resorts, Sandals

were launching a deal to sponsor the West Indies cricket team, and in search, I dare say, of the right sort of publicity, they had invited the world's press to stay. Mixed couples being the order of the day, the appearance of a lot of single men was viewed with some surprise by the normal guests, but all must have gone well for twelve years later the sponsorship is still in place.

On the rest day in the Test Match, Christopher arranged for the chairman's private plane to fly some of us across to St Lucia for lunch and a round of golf. It was tremendous fun. I can't remember whether he wrote our pieces as well. I am sure he will tell you he did, and could have managed it. He has been a great credit to the Hogs and to cricket, one of the real pillars of the club game. And I can't believe he won't take another wicket or two yet.

Written by Johnny Woodcock,
Doyen Cricket Correspondent of The Times *1954-88*
and Editor of Wisden Cricketers' Almanac *1980-86*

* * * * *

After all those years of toiling away bowling into the wind for the Hogs insisting the captain sets 'my field', the countless hours organising cricket matches....playing for somebody else and told them how to organise it! My introduction to Hampshire's Mr Cricket: Right arm over and around the wicket bowler and batsman of immense talent; even if it was in his own mind, well you have to believe don't you and in Christopher Bazalgette you get that in spades. Many congratulations Christopher on a much deserved testimonial, which is lovely recognition of all the years you have put into cricket and the Hampshire Hogs in particular.

We go back some way and it was a Golden Oldies Cricket Festival for the then over 40's that began the friendship. The Festival sponsor was Air New Zealand and its motto was the

3 F's Fun, Friendship and Fraternity, which was a nice angle. Cricket friendships, I think are more far reaching than any other sport I know, but I think our sport is unique almost like actors dressing up for a performance and it is no coincidence that the stage likes dressing up in whites to play cricket and there are more books written about the game than any other sport, including Gette's contribution! I personally had the pleasure with trepidation of organising The Golden Oldies Festival in Brighton in 1986. I was President of the Sussex Invitation League and as such had access to the village grounds within Sussex which helped the festival to flourish.

The festival was held every two years (more time to save up) 1988 went to Brisbane but Christopher and I met in the lead up to the Vancouver event in 1990. We both attended the Festival, which was very well run and the hospitality outstanding. (British Columbia CC toured the UK July 2007) From there Christopher went with the Festival to Christchurch NZ in 1992 and the Birmingham event in 1994. Ever the willing 'horse' he always made himself available to play for other teams in the Festival when they were short and even made the Ist team!

Christopher will have lovely memories of playing for the Auckland Cricket Society, a certain NZ Fingletoads and even the Auckland Police. He does recall a debut at The Valley of Peace, outside Canterbury, South Island NZ which I would like to twin on his behalf with Warnford, which as in dotage and the setting sun those memories will come flooding back, dreaming we are going to do it all over again, richer in mind for having had the opportunity to have done something in life we loved doing. Keep going Christopher: You really deserve a bumper testimonial, keep believing.

Written by Peter Graves, the former prolific batsman for Sussex CCC for many years, and UK Director Golden Oldies Secretariat.

Ivo Tennant who lives in Hampshire and who met Christopher through *The Cricketer*, writes for The *Times* and was Bob Woolmer's ghost writer. In March and April he reported on the biggest sports story of the year (2007). This article was written immediately after learning that Bob Woolmer,v who was coaching Pakistan; had died in Jamaica, in unexplained circumstances, on 18th March.

The professional cricketer by and large has scant interest in the life of his interlocutor. The reporter poses questions and he answers or: sometimes; evades them. But there are exceptions and the most prominent, perhaps, was Bob Woolmer, who has died at an age, 58, when he could still harbour ambitions of becoming the next England coach. He was always considerate, generous and possessing of a genuine interest in any journalist – and his family – he came to know well.

I was fortunate enough to have watched, then known him from the day I obtained his autograph during Folkestone week in 1968, his first season in the game, to interviewing him and dining with him until our last meeting in January.

He ate regularly at what he considered to be the best restaurant in the world, a Portuguese establishment in Cape Town. Would order langoustines and the finest chardonnay produced in the Cape and insist on paying. His conversation was far from restricted to cricket, but he was never happier than returning to the subject of a game he loved. Not for him was there any sense of relief at a stoppage for rain.

He was too generous with his time. Any player could go to his room at any hour for advice: any reporter could email him and get a lengthy response. When Pakistan were involved in the ball-tampering controversy at the Oval last year (2006), Bob was in constant demand from the media. No one can have made so much use of a mobile phone, or, indeed, of all kinds of technology, which he mastered with a childlike interest.

This love of the game shone through in every conversation or practice session he took. Who else would think of transporting a slab of marble around the country for use in the nets? To Allan Donald, the South African pace bowler, he was 'simply the best technical coach around'. Even if Bob was known in his youth, when aspiring to play Test cricket as 'Bobby England'. That was only a reflection of his enthusiasm.

In January 2007 we spoke of the amount of flying he had to do. Bob did not fear that the plane would crash but he appeared that night to have a premonition that he would not live to a great age. He talked about having his ashes scattered at the St Lawrence Ground in Canterbury, the venue he graced with so many cover drives. Then, reverting to his customary optimism, he spoke of the possibility of coaching England, that he would not seek to have his contract renewed by the Pakistan Cricket Board and his hopes of starting his own academy.

Would he have taken the England job? He would have done if made the right offer. For all his experience, his high-earning days with Kerry Packer and as a member of the first breakaway England team to tour South Africa. Bob was not well off. He said that his home in Cape Town was worth no more than a lock-up garage in Central London. He probably worked and travelled more than was good for him and did not care for the constant politicking within Pakistani cricket.

I shall miss his flow of emails, his kindness, his coaching tips to my son and, above all, his zest for life. There was no such thing as a difficult moment with him: the relationship between the star coach and the 'ghost' of his columns and his Autobiography was an even one – even though he had given so freely of his time that sometimes he could not recall that he had made a particular observation. It did not matter because these were usually spot-on. No one cared more about the game, or understood it and those who people it, better than Bob.

Ivo Tennant – Cricket Correspondent for The Times

Luckily, teams have been short on occasions and his services have still been required. Younger Hogs have generously put up with his lack of mobility in the field.

In 2008, Hampshire Hogs Golfing Society took part in their customary four events. The final one of these at Alresford marked our 50th such day. At a dinner after the play, Christopher Van der Noot had a menu designed and Josh Gifford, the former brilliant jump jockey and trainer, entertained guests with a lively speech. The golfing section is open to Hampshire Hogs and friends and aims to raise funds to subsidise young cricketers playing cricket in the summer holidays.

In the autumn, Peter Came invited Christopher to sell the personalised cricket equipment that was marketed under the name Jazzhat Cricket Company. Sadly, Christopher totally failed in this despite contacting clubs and friends around the country. This was a great disappointment as he felt he could repay some of the support Peter had given me.

Early in 2009, Christopher received a telephone call from Australia House asking him to raise an Old Australian team to play Old England on the occasion that the National Trust property Sheffield Park was to be re-opened on the centenary of the third Earl of Sheffield's death.

In the 1890s, Sheffield Park was the ground on which the touring Australians played their first match. The Sheffield Shield became an annual competition in Australian domestic cricket and the Shield was brought over for the match and displayed. Both Dean Jones, who captained the side, and Rodney Hogg were already in the UK and we decided to contact young Australians who were gaining experience as semi-professionals on contract for the summer season. Several of those contacted had to play for their clubs on the Sunday in question, but we were able to raise eight quality players and one other who was on a world tour with his ship (Australian

Navy). The captain agreed to dock at Portsmouth on the Friday and left on the Monday, the day after the match. Three thousand people bought tickets on a glorious day and Old Australia beat Old England by 40 runs. The organisation by the National Trust was superb and the MCC President, Derek Underwood, and his wife graced the occasion.

On our man's own cricketing front, wickets were hard to gain at the beginning of the season and being less supple, he found it harder to make the ball swing. One special scalp was gained in a match for the Hogs against London New Zealand. One of the opposition's opening batsmen was the New Zealand u-19 captain who blasted the Hogs' opening attack to all parts. Christopher was brought on first change and had him lbw off his third ball. Later in the season our man was given the new ball against the Free Foresters, Rupert Cox and Peter Came. Rupert made a great century and Peter made a quickfire 20 before the declaration, but Christopher took four for 70, including the wicket of Rupert and Peter was dropped off the last ball of their innings.

This gave him 36 wickets for the season. 2010 has brought him a few more scalps thus he has reached his career targets of 1400 (1404) for the Hampshire Hogs and in excess of 3800 (3824) in total. Plus one more Test cricketer – John Stephenson (England, Essex and Hampshire) the current MCC Assistant Secretary (Cricket), when John captained Cross Arrows against The Bat & Ball.

Early in the year Christopher made an appointment with Mark Alleyne, the senior cricket coach of the Lord's Indoor School, to discuss the value of 'Trajectory', as good use of this factor (different from Flight) brings wickets – it has been noticeable how Graeme Swann gives the ball more air now and his 'bag' has increased dramatically.

During this year Christopher's legs have become far more painful and his movement considerably reduced. He is now unable to chase any balls that are not hit directly to him in the field, his run up to the wicket when bowling has been reduced to a few strides at walking pace and when he bats he stays at one end, unless he is able 'to walk' a run.

Josh Gifford

By William Tyrwhitt-Drake

I first met Josh back in the 'sixties with my sister, before she married Terry Biddlecombe. Josh and Terry were completely inseparable party animals, both incredibly gifted steeplechase jockeys, very brave and foolhardy and at the pinnacle of their profession. The golden boys of steeplechasing indeed. I was privileged to spend time at the races and afterwards with these two legends.

Josh, his friend David Nicholson and others were very keen on cricket and during the close season, which in those days ran from June until August, the National Hunt jockeys cricket team, wearing the Queen Mother's racing colours, toured the country, raising money for the Jockey's Fund, their own charity for injured riders. I was invited to play for them at various venues around the country. The standard varied but it was definitely not joke cricket. Josh was a determined opening batsman who never gave his wicket away. He didn't have many shots but played with a straight bat and with plenty of courage against the quickies.

He started his own five-day tour around Sussex and Hampshire in the 1980s. We played again the Eton Ramblers at Hook on Friday, followed by the Hogs on Saturday and Robert Green's XI at Itchenor Park on the Sunday. Josh's own club, Findon, hosted the Monday game and if anyone was still standing we finished at Wisborough Green on the Tuesday. Sleep was limited, alcohol was plentiful and quite often the Hog Ball took place on the Friday Night. This was always an all-nighter.

Lots of well known sportsmen took part. Ian Balding, the celebrated trainer of Derby winner Mill Reef; Jock Livingstone, formally a first-class cricketer; Ian Gould and Les Lenham of

Sussex; Godfrey Evans, the legendary England wicket keeper; David Brown, once an England opening bowler, and many others besides.

Josh spent hours on the telephone putting the side together and finding last minute replacements. He loved it and so did we. Many of those players have become lifelong friends. After 20 years, few of us could bend, throw, bowl or catch and the game became quite dangerous for us. So sadly Josh had to call a halt. By now he was playing a lot of golf in much the same style as his opening batting. Nothing extravagant - just straight down the middle and quite effective.

We always play in Guy Harwood's annual tournament. Guy has two bars situated on the course for two pit stops but Josh always managed to nip in for four! Josh retired from riding in 1970, having ridden 640 winners. Some of these were very contentious, such as Hill House, which won the Schweppes gold trophy in 1967. This was a big gambling race.

After many months of scientific testing, the horse was found to manufacture his own speed enhancing drug. Josh won most of the big races although the Grand National, Gold Cup and Champion Hurdle eluded him. He started training immediately he retired from the saddle at Ryan Prices stables, where he had worked for ten years. The fairytale story of Bob Champion recovering from cancer riding Aldaniti, a patched up race horse belonging to him, to win the Grand National, will always be part of racing folklore. He trained the winner of many big races including one of my father's at Cheltenham in 1989.

He finally made way for his son, Nick, in 2003, but he is still never far away from the stables and of course his gold medallist event rider daughter, Tina, is there as well. So the Gifford training establishment is still a wonderful family affair. He is still fit and enjoys his golf and any shooting invitation, as well as watching cricket. He still weighs the same as he did when retiring from the saddle, which, if you saw his appetite, would not surprise you. He has always had huge enthusiasm for life and I have been lucky to spend many happy hours in his company with many loyal friends.

CHAPTER 8

Other Connections

There are nine people who have received Profiles who I came to know through specific occasions that have not fallen into the natural run of the autobiography.

It is sometimes strange that one's paths continually cross for no specific reason, however, as these people have been part of my life and their own names are very well known, I decided their Profile could add an extra dimension to the book. Here is an explanation of how I knew each of them:

The Lord Bramall I first met playing cricket at St Cross in Winchester, he was playing for The Royal Greenjackets against The Hampshire Hogs, he then spoke at The Hogs' Centenary dinner and when he became President of MCC, through my work on *The Cricketer* we often met, it was also fairly natural for me having been in The Brigade of Guards to have an affinity with the General.

General Sir Roger Wheeler and I were educated at Allhallows School in Devon, although he was there later than myself we frequently met over the years playing cricket for the Old Honitonians, as shortly after the end of the Summer term there was always a cricket week. Families would stay in the school and different cricket clubs would be our opponents each day. Roger was a good batsman and an excellent fielder. All his friends knew he would gain honours in the Army and are proud that even though he achieved the most senior rank, he was always the same person with his friends.

Sir Paul Getty, as everyone knows Sir Paul was a great benefactor to cricket, after he created his lovely cricket ground at Wormsley, most cricketers had an ambition to play or be invited to one of his events.

My opportunity came when The Forty Club played their second match at the ground. Due to my disability, it was decided I should be twelfth man, there is no possible chance of playing, I was told. So after lunch I was standing outside the pavilion talking to the great man when the first change bowler in delivering his first ball slipped and twisted both ankles.

Luckily I had not imbibed too greatly at lunch and therefore was able to take the field. I found Sir Paul a very interesting man and a very hospitable one, he will be hugely missed by the cricket hierarchy, no doubt he is already entrenched in the Elysian Fields pavilion.

Sir Tim Rice – I first spoke with him, following conversations with various members of The Heartaches, Sir Tim's cricket team challenging them to play at Broadhalfpenny Down, this was followed by sending him my book called 'THINK-Cricket'. Later I met him on separate occasions, when he played for The Lord's Taverners against The Duke of Richmond & Gordons XI, in which I was playing during their 300th anniversary celebrations and the following match a year later; I happened to be bowling when Sir Tim came to the crease. Although he is always busy, he is always very willing to talk and offer support or advice.

Bill Smith (The Queen Mother's Jockey and Racing Manager for the Royal Family in Dubai) – I met Bill three years ago and see him every morning except when he is in some different country around the world, buying and selling racehorses or attending race meetings. For these days I deliver his papers each day of the week – but not at weekends.

Nick Syrett – To most people Nick is known for being Hon. Secretary for The Wanderers CC for the last twenty six years or for being the Secretary of The Winchester Club in Putney for 27 years. For the sake of my book it is his earlier exploits that we feature and I heard about them through a mutual friend, coincidentally they were both friends of Mike Hawthorn.

I first met Nick through the Cricketer International, as we ran an annual cricket competition for leading Public Schools Old Boys teams and Nick always helped out with the Final, responsible for loudspeaker commentary, but he contributed hugely. Then he brought the Wanderers to Warnford and I knew him even better. His is a great story….

Sir Ron Brierley (New Zealand) is one of cricket's great benefactors, a former President of New Zealand cricket and a kind and generous gentleman to the sport worldwide.

I first heard about his exploits from Swan Richards who is the man whose brainchild is The Crusaders Cricket Club, based in Melbourne, Australia.

They have provided for scholarships for young Australians and they play schools in Australia promoting the game for the young and tours for former quality cricketers. Sir Ron Brierley is a major sponsor for them.

I later met him at a select luncheon at The Oval, when Sir Alec Bedser was being honoured, only six people were present and I had unexpectedly arrived, so I was invited to join them. Many years later I needed some funds for youth sponsorship of Broadhalfpenny Down and Sir Ron was very generous.

Peter Tuke is a friend who has worked tirelessly for cricket, he raised huge funds almost alone for building a new pavilion on Broadhalfpenny Down.

He then organised numerous cricket matches for boys and

girls for many years, in various guises, matching overseas teams and their counterparts in the United Kingdom. This is a tribute to him and the great work he has done for so many people, seldom with the thanks he was due.

J.R.T. 'Trout' Barclay was a former President of MCC, I first met him when he captained the Eton Ramblers against The Hampshire Hogs, over the years I have frequently asked his advice on cricketing matters. With Johnny you are sure to receive the most informed reply and he is so enthusiastic. You would almost certainly see him if you visited Arundel, whether you were playing there or watching a first class match. On occasions he has spoken at the Forty Club Dinner. Johnny Captained the Sussex County Club and was the England coach on overseas tours. Recently he wrote his autobiography *Beyond The Airing Cupboard,*

This is a must read.

He has recently written the Foreword for the 2nd Edition of *Think Cricket*, which follows on from the success of the 1st edition, this was my first commercial book.

Field Marshall Lord Bramall

KG, GCB, OBE, MC, DL JP

By George Gordon-Smith

In more than sixty-four years of service Field Marshall The Lord Bramall rose through every level of command, from a platoon in the Second World War to four-star Commander-in-Chief. He served in the Far East and the Middle East and commanded an armoured division in the British Army of the Rhine at the height of the Cold War before becoming head of the Army and then Chief of the Defence Staff. Six months before the 2003 invasion of Iraq he warned that such a conflict would produce the very display of massive dynamic United States activity that provides one of the mainsprings of motivation for terrorist action in the Middle East – and, far from advancing the 'war against terrorism' it would make matters infinitely worse. And it has.

As a junior officer 'Dwin' Bramall fought with the 60th Rifles in Normandy and Belgium, where he was twice wounded and awarded the Military Cross. In the course of his subsequent wide range of military appointments he developed his thesis on 'indirect military influence', which was to have future implications for the formulation of Britain's foreign and defence policies.

The Falklands experience, in which he was closely involved as Chief of the General Staff and Head of the Army, highlighted the need to look beyond the Soviet threat to Britain's interests around the globe.

As Chief of the Defence Staff 1982-5, he sought to turn the single Service Chiefs away from the Soviet threat towards the growing challenges to Britain's security and national interests arising in the Middle East and Asia.

On his retirement, Dwin Bramall completed fifteen years as a Trustee of the Imperial War Museum, with nine years as its Chairman, a period which covered its most extensive development and expansion, and in 1986 he was appointed Her Majesty's Lord Lieutenant of Greater London.

Given a Life Peerage in 1987 and now as a Cross Bencher in the House of Lords, he continues to question the measures taken for the nation's security and argues for a much closer co-ordination of foreign and defence policy.

Editor's note: Dwin Bramall has been a very good cricketer and I met him playing against the Royal Green Jackets, later he was made President of the Marylebone Cricket Club in 1989, and is a regular visitor to Lord's during Test matches.

General Sir Roger Wheeler

GCB, CBE

By Nigel French
A fellow Honitonian

Roger Wheeler was the most unassuming of successful military leaders but beneath his modest manner was a steely determination which saw him rise to be the Head of the Army.

His father, also a soldier, sent Roger to Allhallows School in Devon where Roger excelled in pretty well everything he tried. He was an avid sportsman and spent four years in the rugby XV, three years in the First Hockey team and two years in the Cricket XI. Captaining the first team in all three sports in his last year, 1961. He also proved a very skilled small bore shooter and rose to be head of the school and not surprising given his later career, was the Senior Under Officer of the schools CCF.

From Allhallows he gained a Kitchener Scholarship to Hertford College, Oxford from where he obtained an MA in Geography and graduated in 1964. He was then commissioned into The Royal Ulster Rifles.

His military career was truly outstanding from its beginning. He was a very humble officer who paid more attention to the welfare of the men under him than many other officers. He was pragmatic, energetic and had a strong vision of the responsibilities each and every promotion vested upon him.

In the early years he served in Borneo and the Middle East but it was when he became seconded to Lord Carver's staff for the Rhodesian talks in 1977 at 36 years old that he came to the attention of the higher command of the time. He also came to the attention of another member of the Carver team, Felicity Hares, with whom he fell in love and married in 1980 having then divorced his first wife with whom he had had 3 sons and a daughter.

As a Battalion Commander he served in Belize, Gibraltar, Berlin, Canada, lending credence to the old army saying which he was to quote many years later, that Army wives never have time to unpack.

In June 1982 immediately following the surrender of the Argentinean troops in the Falkland Islands Roger was sent out as COS of the remaining military Garrison, having been at the MOD during the conflict.

He was Commanding Officer of the 1st Armoured Division in the Rhine for three years finishing in 1990. This stint did enable him to renew his cricketing attachment to the Stragglers of Asia for whom he had played in the past. Roger did not fit the normal criteria for membership of this august touring side which was to "have been in residence for at least two years East of Suez". The Stragglers played a lot of cricket in Germany, mostly against Military establishments, with side tours to Holland until 1994. Roger was an exceptional fielder, bowled "Military Medium" cutters just short of a length with nagging accuracy and his batting was like his military career not flamboyant, but solid and reliable.

From directing military operations in Northern Ireland from 1993-96 Roger swiftly rose from Joint Commander of the UK forces in Bosnia to Commander of the UK Land Forces and then to the top as Chief of the General Staff by 1997 before retiring in 2000. He also served for 5 years as President of the Army RFU and the Army Rifle Association thus continuing his attachment to both sports from his school days.

Roger does not do retirement and he swiftly took on Non Executive Directorships with Thales, Aegis Defence Services, was on the Governing Body of the Serious Organised Crime Agency and in his spare time was Constable of the Tower of London, a Trustee of the Royal Armouries, and more recently became Military advisor to the Chilcot Enquiry.

To those who know him he has a good sense of humour and a love of life which is undiminished with the years.

Nick Syrett

By Paul Lawrence and Denis Jenkinson

Whilst at Bradfield College, Nick Syrett dreamt of playing cricket for Surrey. Alas, this was never to be fulfilled. National Service in the RAF did nothing to raise his hopes. The RAF representative side in the year in which he might have played included five individuals who went on to play Test cricket for England – Ray Illingworth, Jim Parks, Roy Swetman, Fred Titmus and Fred Trueman – and another five who were to secure contracts with five counties. On his only appearance for Fighter Command, he did nothing to improve his chances.

Following demobilisation and several less than satisfactory seasons of club cricket in Surrey, Nick's attention was drawn to motor racing as an alternative weekend pastime. This, while thoroughly enjoyable, was equally unsuccessful. Clearly his great friend and mentor, Mike Hawthorn, had nothing to worry about. However, in 1957 he landed the position of Assistant Secretary of the British Racing & Sports Club.

This was the beginning of what was to become a remarkably successful career as one of the world's most revered race organisers and clerks of the course. Just 12 months later the club's secretary, who was also Stirling Moss's manager, departed – he could no longer afford to do the job – and a desperate search for his successor ensued.

It became apparent that no suitable candidate could afford to do the job either. Several were approached, and Nick was appointed at £750 a year and a Hillman Husky at the tender age of 24.

In 2004, Paul Lawrence wrote *The BRSCC 60 Years* and had this to say about Nick:

'One of the pivotal figures in taking the club to the forefront of the sport arrived in the BRSCC's offices in February 1958 (sic), the young Nick Syrett was already working in the club office and was appointed club secretary, taking over when Ken Gregory resigned his position to concentrate on a full-time role managing the career of Stirling Moss. Syrett had motor sport in his background, as his uncle – Bertie Kensington-Moir – had raced at Brooklands before the war. Syrett was also a friend of Mike Hawthorn and when Hawthorn claimed the 1958 World Championship, a BRSCC member had won the biggest prize in motorsport.

'When Syrett took over, the BRSCC was running around 12 meetings a year and many of them were at Brands Hatch. But more and more circuits were coming into use and, aside from Brands, Crystal Palace, and Silverstone, venues like Oulton Park, Mallory Park, Aintree and Castle Combe were all active. Meanwhile as the 1950s came to a close, Syrett was pushing ahead with ambitious plans to expand dramatically the club's racing programme.

'Back in 1959, the BRSCC was doing well and Syrett was well placed to guide the club into the new decade with an ever-expanding programme of racing at a growing number of tracks. With Nick Syrett at the helm and membership rocketing forward, the BRSCC went into the 1960s on the crest of a wave.

'Syrett's enthusiasm for sports car racing was clear and the club's growing partnership with Brands Hatch would leave it ideally placed to take on the organisation of some of the biggest races in Britain over the coming two decades. Ever the innovator, Syrett delivered a stream of new ideas through the early 1960s. Among them was the first endurance race for saloon cars to be held in Britain, 'The Motor' Six Hours at Brands Hatch. Somewhere along the way, Syrett earned the nickname of 'The Guv'nor,' such was his standing in the sport.'

In July 1967 Nick took on the most ambitious venture of his career, the organisation of the first World Championship sports car race to be held in this country since 1959. The late Denis Jenkinson, Continental Correspondent of 'Motor Sport' magazine wrote in glowing terms: 'The B.O.A.C. 500 – Our best race. It is remarkable, but true, that we have not had a serious motor race, other than Grand Prix events, in Great Britain since 1959; this was brought home forcibly when practice began at Brands Hatch for the BOAC 500. The assembly of car was such that British spectators must have wondered if they were not at Nurburgring, Spa or Le Mans. It seemed impossible that it was in Great Britain, and furthermore it was the final, and critical, round in the Prototype and Sports Car Manufacturers' Championship.

'That vigorous and enterprising club, the BRSCC, with the backing of Sir Giles Guthrie and the British Overseas Airways Corporation, put us back on the international calendar and were rewarded with a really fine race. The only pity was that it was held at Brands Hatch, a circuit that was not really large enough for a race of this calibre and one to which the public seem reluctant to go in vast numbers.

In spite of this the race was a huge success and if Nick Syrett and BOAC have their way it will become an annual classic event.

'Every credit must go to Nick Syrett and BRSCC for putting this country back on the international map with a proper long distance race. Anyone who was going to go to Brands Hatch and changed their minds at the last moment must regret it forever.'

And 'Jenks' in his continental notes column in the same issue of the magazine, wrote: 'That go-ahead club, the BRSCC, under the direction of Nick Syrett, last month took the bull by the horns and made a stand against the bureaucracy of the R.A.C. and F.I.A. on the subject of the capacity limits for long distance racing. When the BRSCC were assured of having most of the people interested in this type of racing at Brands Hatch for the B.O.A.C. race, Syrett called a meeting in London for the day after the race. The object was to discuss this C.S.I. decision and it received immense support......Anyway, all credit to the BRSCC for having the initiative to do something and get people together. If they controlled the sport in Great Britain I am sure that things would be a lot healthier and more efficient, but that is just a matter of opinion.'

And, back to Paul Lawrence in *The BRSCC 60 years*: 'By any standards the 1960s had been spectacularly successful for the BRSCC, membership had boomed, new racing categories had evolved and the club had run race meetings at the very highest level of the sport. Guide by the talented Syrett, backed by a progressive board and ably supported by dedicated enthusiasts across the regions, the BRSCC could rightly claim to be the leading British race organising club of the decade.

'Just as it had gone into the 1960s on the crest of a wave, the BRSCC started the 1970s with an incredible – and justified – outlook of optimism. Early in 1972 there was a significant change in the club's management. After a hugely successful time as executive director, Nick Syrett left the club to take up a position with the Grand Prix Drivers' Association in Geneva. His contribution to the BRSCC cannot be understated and it would be a tough vacancy to fill. 'Nick Syrett was always a towering figure and I always enjoyed working with him', says Stuart Turner, Competitions Manager of the Ford Motor Company and BRCSS Director.'

Syrett soon returned to his first love, rejuvenating The Wanderers Cricket Club and becoming Hon. Secretary, from 1983 to 2009. Motor racing's loss was The Wanderers' gain. He also has been secretary of the Winchester Club in Putney for 27 years.

Sir Ron Brierley

By Christopher Bazalgette

Sir Ron Brierley is arguably New Zealand's most successful businessman and unquestionably the most generous of cricket supporters. Born (1937), raised and educated in Wellington, he attended the prestigious Wellington College, where he joined the New Stamp Dealers Federation.

While still at school, he commenced his first business selling stamps to staff and pupils and continued to develop his love of cricket. His school venture, which was called the Kiwi Stamp Company, was operated from his school desk and set the standard for many of his future trading activities.

Shortly after leaving Wellington College, he formed an aggressive and controversial share market tipping sheet called New Zealand Stocks and Shares. His provocative style earned him a solid following as he developed his personal understanding on the share market. During this time, Sir Ron worked in a clerical position in the insurance industry and studied for accountancy qualifications. Neither lasted very long and he concentrated on his tipping sheet, which was sent unsolicited to all New Zealand listed companies.

In March 1961 he launched R.A. Brierley Investments Ltd. The objects of the company summed up Sir Ron's early aspirations:

To take over or acquire substantial holdings in New Zealand and Australian companies with a view to ultimate participation in management and the re-organisation of their finances.

Investment in companies and industries in which it is believed that rationalisation and mergers are inevitable in the normal course of events.

Participation in selected private companies which are successful but unable to expand. Capital input will increase the value of these companies.

To form a property company to deal in property and maximise wealth creation in this sector.

To trade in Stock Exchange shares with a view to short and medium term appreciation.

R.A. Brierley Investments Ltd was launched with no capital and set about an elaborate but only partially successful campaign to raise share capital. During the early stages of the operation, Sir Ron was the sole share trader and was bookkeeper and main employee for the company. The early stages were not easy but Sir Ron's meticulous approach to business, whereby he researched every purchase decision; projected well into the future the potential benefits of transactions; his ability to think innovatively and his determination to succeed led to a slow growth in investors during the late 1960s.

In 1964 in a typically positive move, R.A. Brierley Investments Ltd purchased Industrial Equity Ltd to provide an opportunity to invest in Australia.

In the '70s and '80s there was considerable growth and consolidation. In 1971 the company became Brierley Investments Ltd and the ongoing strengthening resulted in it joining New Zealand's top 20 companies by 1981. By 1984 this was considered to be the largest company by market capitalisation. Investment expanded in Australia and spread into the USA, United Kingdom and Asia. The sound base established by the company and its directors ensured it survived the 1987 market crash.

In 1990, Sir Ron became founder president of Brierley Investments Ltd and in 2001 he retired from the company. In March of 1990 Sir Ron was appointed to the Board of Guinness Peat Group and remains as chairman of the Board.

Never married though rarely short of female company, Sir Ron likes a glass of good wine and the company of friends. Among many of his friends are a large number of cricketers, officials and supporters who have been fortunate enough to enjoy his hospitality at various cricket grounds around the world.

Sir Ron has had a long and passionate involvement with cricket. He has been a player of moderate ability with the Midland Cricket Club in Wellington. Many cricketers in New Zealand and Australia may not realise how indebted to Sir Ron they are, through his quiet but extensive support for many aspects of the game. For many seasons he was chairman of the New Zealand Cricket Foundation, which provided support for scholarships, cricket pitches and facilities and other worthwhile grassroots projects. Under Sir Ron's guidance, the Foundation developed a solid capital fund and investment portfolio, providing a source of income of great value to cricket in New Zealand. His sound advice and astute chairmanship of the Foundation was renowned and he surely holds the record for the shortest annual general meetings. The Foundation AGM was traditionally held before the AGM of New Zealand Cricket and under Sir Ron's chairmanship was notable for the amount of information provided and the decisions taken in no more than five minutes.

In 1995, Sir Ron was recognised by being appointed president in the New Zealand centenary season. His contribution to the successful completion of a series of cricket dinners and celebrations throughout the country was substantial and his calming presence in a difficult period for New Zealand Cricket was appreciated.

Sir Ron has been a benefactor to cricket in other parts of the world including Australia. He has supported a number of projects ranging from spin bowler clinics to the Cricket in Australia Collection in the State Library of New South Wales.

He is patron of Wellington Cricket Association and the Auckland Cricket Supporters Club. He is a regular visitor to Test matches in Australia, New Zealand and England and frequently hosts former international players at his beloved Basin Reserve in Wellington.

Sir Ron is a quietly spoken, dignified, retiring individual whose generosity and friendship within cricket circles is appreciated and respected. Deservedly knighted in 1987, he has proved to be an extremely astute business leader whose acumen is still serving his shareholders and investors extremely well. Importantly, he retains his love of cricket.

Recently, a one act play was performed in New Zealand which commemorated a very dramatic day in New Zealand cricket. This took place at Johannesburg in 1953. Central characters were the late Bert Sutcliffe and Bob Blair, the fast bowler who took part in a remarkable last wicket partnership after Sutcliffe had been badly hit and batted with his head swathed in bandages. Blair had been advised of the death of his fiancée in a train crash the previous day. Upon hearing of the play, Sir Ron generously ensured that Blair was able to fly from Britain, where he now lives, to attend a performance and to spend a week with friends at the Basin Reserve watching a Test match.

A wonderful gesture from a genuine and much liked benefactor of the great game of cricket.

Peter Tuke

By Simon Tuke (*his son*)

Peter Tuke was born in 1933 in London. He spent his early childhood in Cornwall – a county he has always loved – and was at prep school at St Edmund's in Hindhead during the war. His parents separated when he was very young – a rare and particularly traumatic experience in those days, which meant he spent his wartime holidays in a variety of places from Hindhead to South Wales to St Mawes, looked after for most of the time by a saintly grandmother. By his own admission he was a mischievous child, and Monopoly was eventually banned in the house because he and his older sister, Wendy, got into such terrible disputes over it. He has often commented that whilst the two of them fought like cats and dogs as children, they never exchanged a cross word as adults and were devoted to each other.

From St Edmund's he went onto the less well-known of the two Wellingtons (in Somerset). The plan had been for him to read law at Oxford, but national service intervened, which he served out as an ordinary seaman. He then became an RNVR midshipman, and found himself having such a good time with Mountbatten's fleet in Malta that he contrived to spend the next 27 years in the Royal Navy.

He met his wife Heather in unusual circumstances. Her father was the honorary secretary of the Weymouth Lifeboat for many years, which meant he often gave a bed for the night to a shipwrecked sailors. Peter was sailing a dinghy in Portland Harbour in icy conditions with an inexperienced crew. He told the crew to stay with the boat whatever happened, yet it duly capsized and the crew started swimming for shore. The lifeboat was called and Peter was given refuge by his future father-in-law. Heather and he did not actually meet until some time later, and it was by no means love at first sight; indeed they were both engaged to other people for a while. But finally romance did blossom when Peter was in need of a partner for a social event, and as Heather's maiden name began with H, it was the first he came to in his little black book.

Their first child, Caroline, was born in Malta in 1959. On their return to the UK (the infant Caroline travelling in a miniature hammock crafted by the ship's sailmaker) Peter attended the communications long course at HMS Mercury, where his long involvement with the Broadhalfpenny Brigands began. Their son, Simon, was born in Southsea in 1960.

Peter and Heather started building a first house of their own in the bitterly cold winter of 1962-3; hardly the most fortuitous timing. They lived there until 1972, apart from a tour of duty in Singapore in 1969-70. In 1972 they moved to South Harting, often known as HMS Harting due to the large number of naval families residing there. Apart from a brief spell away, they have lived in the village ever since.

Family holidays were nearly always spent at a remote cottage on Dartmoor: half a mile from the nearest public road; several hundred yards from any road and separated by a river; with no running water, electricity or power of any kind. But with the peerless amenity of "the loo with the view," a doorless outhouse (with red warning flag to indicate occupancy) that was home to the chemical toilet, affording a spectacular vista of the moor, and occasionally of some startled walkers or pony trekkers.

Peter left the Navy in 1980. He joined an exhibition organising company, running their conference division. After a few years he set up his own business, organising conferences, as well as pre-retirement courses for senior executives. As he enters his late 70s, he shows no signs of slowing down, let alone retiring.

He remains equally active around his other interests. He has been a member of several clubs for more than 50 years: MCC, the Naval and Military Club (The In and Out), and Liphook Golf Club. For many years he has run an oil syndicate, which started as a local operation but now numbers some 800 members across several counties. This not only delivers cheaper oil for members, but has also provided many thousands of pounds worth of free oil for local churches.

Peter is a passionate and active supporter of the Liberal Democrats, and has come close on one or two occasions to standing for political office – a prospect that does not fill Heather with joy. He has also long been a vociferous proponent of proportional representation.

Probably Peter's greatest, and most lasting, cricketing achievement has been his role in recent years in the foundation and running of the Broadhalfpenny Down Association (BHDA), and the associated building of the new pavilion.

Broadhalfpenny Down is owned by Winchester College. When the Navy relinquished their lease of the ground, and subsequently closed down HMS Mercury, the Brigands became an independent club in their own right. However, the long-term future of the ground remained uncertain. Peter took on the task of bringing together the various interested parties: Winchester College, the Broadhalfpenny Brigands, Hambledon Cricket Club (who of course had a strong historical link with the ground), Hampshire County Cricket Club and MCC.

The old pavilion, though charming, was entirely inadequate in both size and facilities. Its position also severely limited the playing area and the size of the square. The formation of the BHDA, driven by Peter's enormous energy and diplomatic skills, went hand in hand with plans for a magnificent new structure.

The BHDA has staged many memorable matches, involving famous cricketers as well as the more unexpected, such as inner city youths from both London and Los Angeles. Youth cricket flourishes there, and Hambledon also play quite a few games on the Down. Not forgetting, of course, the Broadhalfpenny Brigands, who continue to thrive, with their naval membership now supplemented by players from many different backgrounds.

Away from the cricket field, Peter has a great love of poetry and verse, with a particular penchant for Belloc and Browning. And he has rarely been known to miss an episode of The Archers.

Sir Paul Getty

By Tim Munton

I have been very fortunate not just to have played for Sir John Paul Getty's XI over the years at Wormsley but also now have the great pleasure to be running cricket operations at the estate. I well remember my first game for Sir Paul back in 1993, which was a year after the inaugural match on the ground, specially created out of the rolling pastures of the family estate in Buckinghamshire. It is one of those places which takes the breath away with its raised bank overlooking the playing area and with the magnificent views down the valley in which the estate nestles. Everything about Wormsley is special, starting with the long downhill drive from the main gates to the ground, which builds up the sense of expectancy. Then, as you come through the woods into the open grassland, you catch a glimpse of the beautiful thatched pavilion and your spirits soar.

It doesn't matter how many times I visit the ground, I have to stop and take in the view between the pavilion and the marquee and consider how lucky cricket is to have been a passion of the late Sir Paul. He was a man of great humility, as understated as the ground itself. As one of the most notable philanthropists of this era, his generosity was directed at many causes, charities, institutions and people. Many will know how his large donation to MCC made the rebuilding of the Mound Stand possible, but what they may not appreciate is the breadth of his support to the game. His backing of cricketing charities, for instance, in particular The Lord's Taverners and the PCA's Benevolent Fund, through events held at Wormsley.

Many of my professional colleagues have been fortunate

enough to host events in their benefit and testimonial years. The fact that so many professionals, both retired and current, were so keen to come and play for him at Wormsley underlined the affection in which he was held in all quarters of the game. And when *Wisden Almanac*, the bible of the game, was put up for sale, Sir Paul stepped in to buy it and guarantee its long-term future as well as that of the Wisden cricket monthly magazine (now the *Wisden Cricketer*).

I always looked forward to the varied array of interesting people at Wormsley during JPG XI matches. At the start, Brian Johnston was 'ground host' before being succeeded by Colin Ingleby-Mackenzie. Here were two of the great characters of the game, warm men who made everyone feel welcome and introduced you to many distinguished people you might be reluctant to approach - the likes of Denis Compton, Keith Miller, Mick Jagger and John Major. But it wasn't all about the great and the good, as Sir Paul and his wife, Lady Victoria, liked to host people from all walks of life. I really enjoyed the fact that cricket had so clearly given him so much pleasure and happiness in the second half of his life. The story goes that he was introduced to the game by Jagger when the pair met in a London clinic and having educated Sir Paul through watching Test matches on the TV, he then introduced him to the home of cricket, Lord's, which sealed his affection and enthusiasm for the game.

Another of Sir Paul's great passions was his collection of books. The library which houses them is a short walk from the ground and has been a favourite pastime at Wormsley for many guests attending matches. The stunning collection includes Charles I's prayer book with the words "Dum Spiro Spero" inscribed by Charles himself. "While I breathe, I hope," is the translation, somewhat ironic as he was beheaded. Other highlights of the collection are vivid medieval manuscripts dating as far back as the 12th century;

the first edition of Caxton's printed Canterbury Tales; Anne Boleyn's Psalter; and the first folio of Shakespeare's Comedies, Histories and Tragedies.

As well as his passion for cricket and the arts, Sir Paul (and Lady Getty) took delight in their gardens and the restoration of the magnificent walled garden was a favourite project for them both. This is a fabulous setting for a champagne reception before moving on to the ground for lunch or the start of play. Typically, Sir Paul wanted all those who were interested to see both this and the library. And that is how I shall remember him: one of the kindest of men who was only too happy to share much of what he had. Cricket is very lucky that Sir Paul Getty fell in love with our great game and few are aware just how much we owe thanks to him for – which I dare say is just how he liked it....

Please look at their website: www.jpgettytrust.org.uk.

Sir Tim Rice

By John Barclay

Leicester Forest Service Station, astride the M1, will not strike many as a place of creativity. Indeed, it was not for this reason I turned off the motorway. I was tired after a lot of driving, in need of a rest and a cup of coffee to liven me up. I sat for a while on my own at a table overlooking the surging evening rush hour. Sipping my coffee and recovering as I did, my thoughts turned to Tim Rice. I wondered whether he had ever tried to complete a work in such an unpromising and uninspiring atmosphere. Could genius possibly be inspired by the combination of the traffic roar and relentless music blaring from the internal system? Probably not and yet, by the same token, Tim is an unusual chap and I felt it not impossible that a masterpiece could emanate from outlandish circumstances.

I have never been sure how great lyricists and musicians put words and music together without falling out with each other. What comes first, the words or the music? The trick, I imagine, must be in the partnership, the meeting of minds, the empathy.

It was only quite late in life that I came to realise that lyrics really are important and appreciate how they need to fit the tune and so give satisfaction and joy to the listeners. For ages I thought only the melody mattered.

That must have been before 'Joseph' first appeared on stage. All of a sudden we had a strong story – a familiar one from the Old Testament – music that was jolly and tuneful, accompanied by witty and descriptive words. I took the family to see it at the Palladium some years ago when the highlight was Jason Donovan (Joseph) soaring high above the audience on a precarious device. This added to the excitement of the show and was particularly appreciated by my daughter, Georgina, whose early years had been dominated by episodes of 'Neighbours.'

There is little doubt that Tim, notwithstanding his cricketing prowess and great love of the game, knows as much about pop and popular music and, for all I know, every other type of music, than most people still living. He knows the people and the culture and is an encyclopaedia when it comes to names, dates and songs. What, of course, Tim does have, which plenty of people do not, is loads of wit and charm. He's fun. Apart from that he is very tall and he has the most marvellous voice which must have kept him out of trouble right from the beginning.

His voice, knowledge and charm must have opened the door to broadcasting and game shows, my favourite being 'Just a Minute' with Nicholas Parsons. Although he is quite competitive, I suspect Tim has never actually won the show, although he just may have done once on a very good day and with the help of the other contestants. I suppose Tim would have made a very capable game show host on 'Strictly Come Dancing' or that sort of thing. But in all truth I think he's a bit above all that. He does have a touch of class - although not as a batsman or bowler.

Tim loves cricket. The two have been close companions in the past. For many years Neville Cardus wrote about music and cricket in the Manchester Guardian and captured the atmosphere of both pursuits with prose that has scarcely been equalled since. Tim always claims with modesty that in the cricketing department both skill and co-ordination passed him by when talent was shared out. I suspect he was a bit better than that, but have yet to see evidence to suggest otherwise. Possibly he was a fair player in his younger days. But I doubt it. I prefer to think that he wasn't much good and indeed he is quite proud of his slender ability. Lack of ability does at least give others a chance to shine.

I am aware of how turbulent and precarious it must be to climb up the greasy pole. There must have been hours spent listening to pop songs and popular music, many a B-side to fend off and out-and-out stinkers to cast aside. And yet I feel that the product of all this has been words and ideas set to music giving us rhythm, metre and much wit; a touch of genius, in fact, for which the world is most grateful. I imagine that Tim's life is rich with words and melody which have helped to shape our culture and perhaps even burrow into our psyche.

Bill Smith

By Christopher Bazalgette

To rise from a small boy who loved horses from the age of nine to become the Queen Mother's jockey and then proceed to be a leading trainer, without influence or sponsorship, shows the power of single determination, courage and ability. This is a remarkable story of dedication, battling everything life throws at one and persevering through injury after injury to an ultimate goal.

Bill Smith started riding at the age of nine, the competitiveness was inborn as his father was a racing cyclist, but the nearest link to horses was the family home was at Shepperton, not far from Kempton Park. For the next six years he showed horses, show jumped and rode in gymkhanas.

Then his first step into the horse-racing arena, he was accepted for apprenticeship at Fred Rimell's stables at Kinnersley, but this was not to be for he was desperately homesick and returned home, home was now at Hayling Island in Hampshire.

Needing a job, he joined Moss Bros as a salesman. Being a bright young man he learnt a lot, he grew up and learnt about people talking with their customers. Eighteen months passed, his real love of horses still beckoned and he resigned and went to work in some riding stables outside Portsmouth.

He was now a young man with an ideal to pursue, stronger and determined to succeed. He managed to persuade a client that he should ride for him in a point-to-point, initially he was left twenty lengths at the start and then he fell off the horse two fences from home.

Then at Hackwood Park in a Hunt race he won, beating one of the first girls permitted to ride against men in English

Points. Bill now was offered and took the job as assistant to the Hampshire Trainer, John Stuart Evans.

He then won again but it was still early days and although he was gaining regular rides, on returning to stables on the Sunday mornings, he wasn't asked how had he had got on, on the day before but at which fence had he fallen. Still aged eighteen he rode his first winner 'under rules' for John Blake; the horse was a three-year-old called Silver Mead and the race was an all aged selling plate, at Taunton. It was his only win as an amateur and he beat a future colleague Ali Branford.(This information from *Jockeys of the Seventies* by Tim Fitzgeorge-Parker).

John Blake had his horses in training with Bill Marshall, whose stables were then at Ogbourne, near Marlborough. Mr Marshall had been at Taunton to see him win in the seller, this was another step up the ladder, as he asked Bill to ride his horse Harlech Lad, but insisted he turned professional first. Bill was to win four novice hurdles on that horse and then stayed on as the Marshall stable jockey for four seasons, this produced fifty plus winners.

Now he was retained by Bill Marshall, Les Kennard and David Tatlow and meant lots of travelling as he rode for Marshall in London meetings, Tatlow in the Midlands and Kennard in the West Country.

Such horses as St Patrick's Blue, Stradivarius and Silver Mead. He also won the Irish Sweeps Hurdle on Kelanne and called his present home after him.

He never schooled any of the horses except one for Tatlow, which refused, never to be asked again.

Fate again played into Bill Smith's hand – Edward Courage gave him a few rides when his stable jockey, Johnny Cook broke his leg – so Bill rode Spanish Steps to win the SGB Chase and he also won the Stone's Ginger Wine Champion Chase on Royal Relief: at the same National Hunt Festival

Ken White was concussed, so Fred Rimell asked him to ride Zarib in the Daily Express Triumph Hurdle and again he won.

The Grand National followed and he rode Bright Willow into seventh.

Bill must have kept himself very fit and now it was to pay off, as suddenly disaster struck, he was cantering down to the start, towards the end of the season at the Devon & Exeter meeting when his horse slipped, stumbled and fell, breaking his jockey's left knee and leg. But young bones mend fast and in six months he was back as stable jockey for Fred Rimell, replacing Terry Biddlecombe. He stayed at Kinnersley for two seasons, not the happiest of partnerships, but Bill took his opportunities. The first season he won The Champion Hurdle on Comedy of Errors and came second in The Irish Sweeps Hurdle, the second season they won the Sweeps, but were beaten by Lanzarote in The Champion Hurdle, he was blamed for Comedy's defeat, but won another Champion Chase on Royal Relief. When Terry Biddlecombe retired, Bill started riding for Fulke Walwyn and the following season became first jockey for the famous Saxon House stable, as Royal jockey for Her Majesty the Queen Mother.

Bill stated 'This appointment started badly, on an outside ride at Fontwell Park my horse slipped on the flat, killing itself, cracking my pelvis and shoulder blade and causing severe internal bruising' – the horse was appropriately called 'Shattered'.

But he was only out for three weeks and despite having a sketchy season on a poor team of horses, he won the Schweppes Gold Trophy on the Queen Mother's Tannuz – one of the best hurdlers he ever rode.

Bill remarked 'I cannot tell you how much it meant to me being her jockey, it was fantastic winning for the Queen Mother'.

Another great moment for Bill was at Ascot partnering Sunyboy to win the Queen Mothers' 300th winner under National Hunt rules. But for two bad mistakes he reckoned he would have won the 2-mile Champion chase at Cheltenham, on Game Spirit for her.

Bill could not praise Fulke Walwyn more, although it took some time for them to blend. He really knows how to gain the best out of horses and will discuss them with the jockey, he was always very loyal to them both, Bill commented 'It gives you heart and makes the job really worthwhile'.

He then finished third and fourth in consecutive Grand Nationals on Spanish Steps.

Bill rode in six Hennessey Gold Cups, starting in 1972 on Notification and then consecutive years from 1976 through to 1981, he came second on Fort Devon in 1977 to Bachelor's Hall, losing by a neck, even though he carried the top weight. In 1981 he won on Diamond Edge owned by a West Country vet called Sam Longbridge.

Again he was on the favourite and this time he won by half a length, Diamond Edge was a very popular win and brought his trainer Fulke Walwyn his seventh success in the race.

Amazingly for a National Hunt jockey, during 1970 and 1971 he had fifty plus rides on the Flat for Bill Marshall, actually being able to reduce his weight to 8 stone 5lbs. Initially he used his stick (whip) too much, but in time learnt that it was not so necessary.

Bill Smith rode 501 winners in his racing career of which sixty three were for The Queen Mother, which makes him second on the list of Royal Jockeys, his idol David Mould was top of the list.

When he came to retire he bought a property of ten acres at Hambledon with an American style barn and many boxes.

One day talking to Sheikh Ahmed, the youngest of the four brothers, he asked if I knew of any Arabian racehorse that was for sale and/or if there was any trainer spare. I replied that although I knew of none for sale, I would find some and as for a trainer I would do that as well.

So it transpired that in January 1992 I bought the first three Arabs for Sheikh Ahmed and by the end of June, had bought 50 more for his brother HRH Sheikh Mohammed bin Rashid al Maktoum.

From there over the next few years I bought horses in vast numbers from all around the world: America, Russia, South America, Turkey and across Europe.

It was around that time there was a relaxation of quarantine regulations for export of horses from the UAE to Europe. Previously they could travel out there but not return. It had always been a vision of Sheikh Mohammed that there should be racing in Dubai and with that in mind he did just that.

Spending a major part of the winter out in Dubai through the nineties and seeing the racing develop was an amazing period and one that never could be repeated. At the same time my training of Arabian horses for the Maktoum family really shot forward and at a high I had a little short of 2000 head of horses around the world. A major team made up of brood mares in the USA, UK and France who produced runners, the best of these going on to Dubai to race there. Leading breeder titles, Champion owners particularly in the USA were a measure of their success.

This was also a time of the Middle East interest in Endurance racing where a horse and rider, the same horse all day, compete up to a 100 miles in a day. It all started in Dubai with an extraordinary Camel v Horse race over 25 miles in a straight line where 28 horses competed against 450 camels! It was an amazing sight where every Sheikh in the UAE attended having lunched in a tent the size of Wembley stadium.

Sheikh Mohammed's daughter won with The Boss coming

second, the first 6 home were horses all USA bred that I had bought through the winter. The winning horse and camel were gifted to the President of the UAE, HH Sheikh Zayed al Nayan! So started another experience of travelling the world competing in and winning World and Open European Championship titles for the UAE teams being Chef D'equipe several times and being 'lucky' enough to be in the right place at the right time.

They say it is better to be born lucky than rich! I, certainly was not born rich but have been incredibly lucky in my life. I had a conversation with Brough Scott that proved to be lucky in forming my second career after being a jockey.

Brough was a Director of the International Racing Bureau who were running the every day racing arrangements of four brothers from the Middle East, they were looking for someone who knew their way around a racecourse, could handle themselves with a Royal family and knew something of the ways of racehorse owners.

It was from here I began an incredible 25-year job with the ruling Family of Dubai, in particular with H.H. Sheikh Mohammed bin Rashid al Maktoum.

As Racing Manager for the al Maktoum family I have been lucky enough to travel the world to almost every racecourse that matters and meet and see things to which most people can only dream.

Being part of the early development of racing in Dubai alone is an unbelievable high. Moreover the present Maydan racecourse (Dubai) is so far removed from the early days and those racecourses I have seen in USA, Canada, Australia, Hong Kong and all around Europe, it is the most amazing sight, but no more than you would expect than from HH Sheikh Mohammed, Ruler of Dubai and the biggest racehorse owner in the world.

For the last 17 years I have been training Arabian racehorses from my farm in Hampshire. We have had some major successes such as the French Derby, the German Derby, other major races in Europe and in the United Kingdom, plus three leading trainer titles. It has all been great fun, as a hobby I have Show Hunters and have owned the winners of the Lightweight, Middleweight and Heavyweight Hunters of the Year at The Horse of the Year Show. I still hunt twice a week through the winter and have been Master of the Hursley Hambledon Hunt for the last ten years.

However, my proudest moment was probably when my daughter rode for the British Endurance team in the World Championships at Jerez, she has represented England in several team championships, but now finds her hands full with her twin daughters.

This profile is a result of Bill Smith talking with Christopher Bazalgette.

J.R.T. "Trout" Barclay

By Andrew Longmore

I first met Johnny Barclay at school. He was at Eton, I at Winchester and we were opposing captains for the annual two-day fixture in June. If I remember right, the match ended in a rather dull draw, partly because of the rain, mainly due to Winchester's slightly negative tactics. We had been heavily beaten for the previous two years and so regarded a draw as quite an achievement. It was the sort of stalemate that Johnny abhorred when he became captain of Sussex.

Even back then, when we were just two toffs enjoying our cricket – "such fun, don't you think?" as he might say - there was something intense and purposeful about the way Johnny tackled the game. He was already an assured and innovative captain, as if preparing for the leadership roles which were to come his way, at Sussex and later as manager of England. He was once or twice talked of as a potential England captain, in a Brearley-esque sort of way. If he was not quite a good enough batsman or bowler to warrant a place in an international side, two aspects of his game were world class: his slip catching and his captaincy.

A few months ago while sitting on a bench in the May sunshine watching Eton play Charterhouse, Johnny recalled those early days. "I was obsessed, ambitious and I wanted to captain Sussex," he said. I captained Sussex under-19s but never with the confidence or the inspiration that marked Johnny's leadership on the field. A tour of India with the England Schools team in 1969 highlighted our different attitudes. I was selected as the second wicket keeper, Johnny as vice-captain and, almost before we had left Heathrow, the squad of northern comprehensive schoolboys and southern public schoolers had subconsciously split into two groups, one of confirmed amateurs, the other of neo-pros. Among the latter were Jimmy Foat and Andy Stovold, who both played for Gloucestershire, Geoff Miller, Derbyshire and England (and goalkeeper for Chesterfield FC Boys as he regularly reminded us) Grahame Clinton (Surrey) and Alan Butcher (Surrey and England) and JRT.

They were already professionals in all but name. The rest of us were still coming to terms with being very little fish in a very deep pool. Had we played every one of the five Tests against India to a conclusion we would have won the series 4-1. As it was we lost it 1-0, our sole defeat coming on a wickedly turning pitch in Jamshedpur when the Indians played three leg-spinners and, frustrated by not being able to bowl them out in the first three Tests, we decided to put them in. By the time we had returned to England after six weeks travelling by train and taxi round the whole of that vibrant continent we had all grown up, as people and cricketers, and JRT had eaten enough scrambled eggs and drunk enough tea to last a lifetime. The trip proved to be the highlight of my cricketing career, just the beginning of Johnny's, barely worth a mention in his wonderfully whimsical autobiography, Life Beyond the Airing Cupboard. I knew cricket was to be part of my life, not the whole of it.

One of the great delights about Johnny is that he has never pretended to be someone he is not. It's hard to hide a background when three initials appear on the scorecard each day, the last of them concealing the family name, Troutbeck, and even harder to hide an upbringing on the playing fields of Eton in a hard-bitten county dressing-room. Just ask Michael Atherton, Manchester GS and Cambridge University, who writes a typically thoughtful and amusing foreword to the autobiography, or, for that matter, Peter Roebuck, a Millfield scholar thrust into the Somerset dressing-room of Viv Richards, Joel Garner and Ian Botham. Roebuck wrote with perception and humour about "Trout" in his book of cricketing essays, Slices of Cricket, vividly recalling the jousts between Botham and Barclay on the county fields. Knowing full well that the mighty all-rounder could resist everything but tempting little off-spinners, Barclay would bring himself self-consciously into the fray, scatter his fielders to all parts and, more often than not, emerge the bowed and bloody victor of the contest. "Such fun, don't you think?"

Johnny never lacked courage on a cricket field, but Roebuck also captured another priceless JRT quality, his ability to get on with pretty well everyone anywhere at any time. Genghis Khan on one of his grouchier days might be regarded as only "fairly nice," Roebuck memorably writes, but an innate curiosity and a deep benevolence towards other humans has made JRT a hugely affable and uncomplaining companion, and, during England's torrid post-apartheid tour to South Africa and Zimbabwe, a slightly eccentric ambassador for English cricket.

Our paths did not cross much after our initial schoolboy skirmishes. But I watched his career, as if living out my own through the county scores in the newspaper, and urged the England selectors to take a chance with him during some of the darker days of the 'eighties. Anyone who could bring the best out of Imran Khan and Garth Le Roux on dank afternoons at Hove and drag Sussex to the brink of their first County Championship title had to be worth a go, I reasoned. Besides, my own cricketing prowess would have been heightened immeasurably if he, my equal just a few years before, had become captain of England. It was probably best for both of us that the selectors resisted the temptation.

After he had retired, we met on a train once, by accident. Johnny had become Director of Cricket at the newly established Arundel Castle Cricket Foundation, a charity which uses cricket to educate and enrich the lives of underprivileged children, and talked pretty well non-stop throughout the 40-minute journey. He had not changed one iota, I thought. Everything was still such fun. I did not know then about the struggles he was facing in his own life, with the death of his wife, Mary-Lou, and the continuing struggles with his inner demons. Still, like many encounters with Johnny, it brightened an otherwise routine day.

So, back to our bench in the Eton sunshine and the sense of a past returning gently into focus. Johnny rarely answers questions; like his batting his conversation is full of deflections and quick singles. His effervescence is, I suspect, a sham, but back in the gilded close of his youth, surrounded by friends, Vic Cannings, his old school coach, now 90 odd and sharp as a pin, John Rice, the former Hampshire stalwart and Eton's head coach, Patrick Eagar, the greatest of all cricketing photographers, Stephen Chalke, the writer and publisher, and Richard Montgomerie, the former Sussex pro, he was in his element. "Such fun, don't you think?"

Andrew Longmore is a senior sports writer for the Sunday Times. *He captained the Old Wykehamists to victory in the Cricketer Cup in 1982 and played two first-class games for Oxford University.*

CHAPTER 9

Older Friends

Looking back on a lifetime of cricket and the stars one met many times over, it is extremely hard to choose whom to single out to be profiled. Once the choice has been made, the author suddenly realises there are many who deserve special accolades who have not been mentioned.

Personal friends such as Bill Edrich, whom I have mentioned briefly elsewhere in this book and who, like Denis Compton, his Middlesex twin, really knew how to enjoy himself off the field as he did on it. Bill had been a fighter pilot during the 2nd World War, winning the DFC. He was not unknown to arrive for a match in dinner jacket and go out and score a ton. Bill loved life and the girls and had enough chat-up lines to fill the Albert Hall. Once on holiday on Corfu, we had visited a topless beach in the boat. When it was time to leave, Bill was seen still chatting up a young girl oblivious that his transport had left and was 100 yards away from shore. Every night he would be supping ouzo into the early hours but by 9 a.m. next day would be fresh for the next venture.

Tom Graveney was elegance personified – he has grace and charm and always the same friendly spirit. Like Derek Underwood he has sold artificial pitches and has also coached the young and been very keen on horse racing.

Brian Close, the bravest of the brave, one of the youngest of cricketers to play for England, fielding close to the wicket or facing the most ferocious fast bowler without helmet or protection. When he was hit, he did not show it. Always controversial, a wonderful captain, who, on account of losing the captaincy of Yorkshire, moved to Somerset, He became godfather to Ian Botham's son Liam, and is much respected by Ian.

Godfrey Evans – Godders – was another who knew how to party. Following his retirement from the game, he ran a pub near Petersfield. Godders was a regular visitor to The Cricketer's Club off Baker Street and always attended the El Vino's dinner. Godders had many a fine tale to tell about his cricketing days for he had been a wonderful wicket-keeper and a gutsy batsman.

I knew John Snow because he advertised his cricket tours in *The Cricketer*. He was quiet and reserved, but put a ball in his hand and he became a fast, hostile bowler who had been very successful spearheading England's attack. John is a great family man who has now retired from business.

Colin Ingleby-Mackenzie went on to captain Hampshire, leading them to the county championship title in 1961. He was an inspired leader. His players would do anything for him, such was his charismatic personality. He had boundless energy, often burning the candles at both ends. One wonders if he found time to sleep. On one occasion, when Hampshire had beaten Oxford University, he and his kindred spirit Leo Harrison, hurriedly changed into morning coats and sped off to Royal Ascot, where they had been invited to join Stanhope Joel, millionaire racehorse owner and breeder, in his box and move on afterwards to dinner at the Compleat Angler in Marlow. After being well fed and watered, they left at about 4.30 am to drive back to Southampton where they were staying with Desmond Eagar, arriving at 7 am, just in time to get into their beds with their clothes on before being unceremoniously hauled out again by Desmond, who asked them if they had slept well. Unknown to them, he had heard them return and when they answered in the affirmative, he told them he knew they had only just come back.

He made them get up and ferried them to Bournemouth for a match. Colin slept all day until someone shook him, saying urgently, 'Skipper, you're in.' He picked up his bat and proceeded to make a century in 61 minutes, the fastest century of the season! Colin won a prize of £100 and the Lawrence Trophy. Later, he was made president of Hampshire, which was followed by the honour of becoming president of MCC. Unlike his predecessors, his period of office was for two years instead of one. Colin also excelled at golf, becoming captain of Sunningdale in 2000.

Gordon Greenidge was an individual whom I managed for three years. He was one of the greatest opening batsmen, as was his partner, Desmond Haynes, for West Indies. Gordon had a philosophy on life and cricket that was far more astute than one would have imagined at his age. His delivery of speech was also unique in that it was similar to someone who stuttered. Part way through a sentence he would stop and after a pause he would pronounce words of wisdom. Wherever he went he had a squash ball with him, gripping and relaxing and strengthening his wrists. For an international cricketer, he was very kind and thoughtful — after a benefit game I had organised for him — with a prize of a case of champagne for the most sixes hit in an innings, of which he was a likely winner — I asked him afterwards why I had not been dispatched out of the park. He replied, 'You had dismissed five of my mates and I wasn't going to be the sixth.' I knew it was his way of thanking me for running the match. None of us was in any doubt that each ball could have disappeared had he so decided to hit out.

He also told me that when he went out to bat, his approach was to survive the first ball, then an over, followed by an hour etc. but the lesson was that he set goals for himself in manageable portions, and that young batsmen should do the same.

Gordon's first love was his wife and family. He doted on them all and was very proud of the children. I hope he has rid himself of the injuries that always appeared when on overseas tours after the Test matches had finished. These usually meant he had to miss the end of the tour and return home.

Many of the Hampshire cricketers I knew well, having travelled on their coach to Bournemouth when they played at Dean Park. This started when I was aged 11 and as one grew up they would introduce you to others and the opposition. Apart from the West Indian cricketers already mentioned, I got to know Andy Roberts, Malcolm Marshall, Wes Hall, Deryck Murray and Jimmy Adams.

I made friends with Sunil Gavaskar, Ravi Shastri and 'Jimmy' Amarnath, Later, I met Sanjay Manjrekar, who told others I had beaten him for pace – I was in fact the slowest bowler he had ever faced.

After 32 years dealing with cricketers every day, I fear I have missed out some special people, I hope I may be forgiven. Even now when playing in a match I wake of a morning and count the minutes until we start. I imagine how I might take a wicket – I have a good imagination – and the bag is carefully packed. Kit should be clean – my mother told me, 'Even if you are no good at playing you can look like a cricketer,' and I always try to arrive early.

CHAPTER 10

Physical Rehabilitation and Maintenance

By Christopher Bazalgette

Courtesy of Ian T.A.Jeffery M.B.S., F.R.C.S. , Naill A.K.Flynn M.B ChB, F.R.C.S., and Wendy Rofe M.C.S.P. and Health Professional Council

This 'life' story would not be complete without an explanation of how I recovered and was able to continue to play sport, although I endured major injuries to my knees.

Initially I had planned to have a career in the Army, only just prior to being examined before a Regular Commissions Board it was found necessary for a cartilage to be removed from my left knee. Soon after, having recovered, a further examination resulted in another operation to remove my kneecap, which had become diseased. During my recovery I fell and the knee had to be opened across the same cut on two separate occasions to re-structure my ligaments.

Finally, when it seemed there was 'light at the end of the tunnel,' the muscle (inter fascia lata strip) that goes from the femur (above the knee) over the knee to the tibia (below the knee) came away, and a fourth cut had to be made across the knee – to repair the muscle and reconnect to the lower bone. This major surgery episode took two years. It was then that I was invalided out of the Army with a 50 per cent disability pension. I started in civvy street coaching cricket, but at the end of the summer term I needed further hospitalisation in Yorkshire for internal stitching of the knee. When I had left hospital, the medical team said if I trained steadily I could look forward to about ten years of sport.

After three years of building muscle I was able to resume playing rugby and actually played for a further 12 years until, aged 35, I cracked my neck, I was warned that if I continued with rugby I would put at risk playing cricket in later life as more problems were likely to occur.

So I gave up playing rugby.

I had resumed playing cricket, one year after taking up rugby again. At first I was unable to bowl, as the leading leg was my left leg. Then I needed a clean-out of the left knee joint.

However, there was only a temporary delay before sport was resumed. For all this period my right leg had borne the brunt of the strain. It was to be 22 years after the earlier surgery that a new surgeon removed the media cartilage from my right knee – luckily for me this brilliant man knew micro surgery and being a sportsman was aware of the need for care. Ian Jeffery was a former front row rugby forward and keen skier and such was his expertise that I resumed sport a month later. Ian was an innovator in terms of knee ligament reconstruction and had brought arthroscopic surgery to Portsmouth in 1982.

I was to have two more arthroscopy operations to my left knee in 1997 and 2005. Each time I was in hospital for less than a day, which meant recovery was even quicker. Ian became a friend and his experience and expertise has made a huge difference to my physical state.

Ian has recently retired, but his work had been carried out alongside another sporting friend and surgeon – Naill Flynn. This was appropriate for my cause as he has been a really good cricketer. At school he represented his county and played for the Royal Corps of Transport when in the Army. When training in Bristol he played cricket for Clifton and rugby for Berkshire. After university he played cricket for the Free Foresters and Grannies (another of my clubs) and he even made a century at Broadhalfpenny Down.

After six months, following a serious injury, he trained in orthopaedics in the Wessex region with specialist fellowship training in the then rapidly developing field of reconstructive knee surgery, and he has led the Portsmouth knee surgery group for the last decade. He is widely published and an internationally acknowledged expert in the rarefied field of knee kinematics.

Naill has been advising me in regard to the next operation I will require, which will be a replacement knee, as for the last four years I have been 'bone on bone.'

The recovery and convalescence after each operation was minimalised due to another expert. Someone who has helped so many sportsmen and sportswomen, of all ages from five years to 85, all wishing to recover from injury and/or operations. My angel was - and is – the super qualified Wendy Rofe – M.C.S.P. and Health Professional Council. Her 20 years experience included training at Farnham Park Rehabilitation for four years in sports medicine and fitness classes, with further training at Heatherwood hospital at Ascot and St Mary's hospital. This has made her a leading professional in the science. I have attended her unit – The Portsmouth Sports Injury Clinic – on and off for 20 years-plus.

In the beginning it was once a week for the knees. Then she treated my back and neck, shoulders, arms and again various parts of my legs – a pulled hamstring was even cured in four days. I was always asking the impossible, but Wendy regularly lowered the barriers.

The unit has five couches and a wonderful support team who are no less dedicated, working non-stop from 6am in the morning until 8 pm. Their motto is 'no pain, no gain.' Every time you visit you will see others who still want to play their sport and return to Wendy for treatment. They also offer aqua pool and back classes, treating 160 patients a week for their backs. I cannot rate them them more highly. What is more, they have never had to advertise and if you ask very nicely the team will fit you in, even when they are fully booked – which is ALWAYS.

There is one further factor that fits into this chapter. My back has caused me lots of pain and I was contacted by representatives of a company called Ecoflow of Liskeard in Cornwall, who supply magnet therapy. The range of products at the time was mainly wrist straps. Now, due to its amazing success, there are many different sized products.

I was given a wrist strap for the sum of £50, and then was told I had three months trial, after which 85 per cent would be returned if I wasn't completely satisfied. Nothing happened to me for three weeks and then one morning I awoke and my back pain was no more. So I was able to cancel physio. The result was great. I even took the strap off to test if I still suffered pain. Within 24 hours it was still there and so back went my strap. Hours later I was OK. I became a representative and sold hundreds, with amazing results, confounding even many sceptics, I think we had five failures out of some 200 sales. Now, years later, I no longer sell them but my dog has a collar and I have my wrist strap. Why do they work? The negative reverse polarity encourages blood flow and the special metal retains the magnetism, unlike those bought from the chemist which usually lose power.

Large magnets are used in hospitals!

APPENDIX 1

Special Hampshire Hog Friends et al

Peter Came

Peter Came, born in Aldershot in 1963, is the grandson of R.W.V.Robins, who captained Middlesex and England, and son of Brigadier Ken Came, who played for The Army, Free Foresters and Hampshire Hogs. Peter inherited the natural talent of both his father and grandfather, being very capable at each of cricket's disciplines. Sadly, he lost both parents at an early age. They would have been very proud of him. As a friend, Peter will always be supportive.

Peter is a professional amateur who will give of his best and expect everybody else to do likewise. He is an organiser, businessman and an all round sportsman. He is a champion of the young and vulnerable.

He played for Bradfield College first XI 1979-81, captained Hampshire u-19s in 1981 and 1982, and played for Hampshire second XI and for Hampshire u-25s. He has represented Bradfield Waifs for 27 years in the Cricketer Cup, which they won in 1997, 1998 and 2005, and has been the leading Waifs wicket taker and run-scorer in *The Cricketer* Cup. A Free Foresters and Hampshire Hogs committee member, he has toured South Africa, Argentina and Channel Islands, and played for MCC. As of 2010, he has scored more than 140 centuries. He is a keen footballer and golfer.

In March 2004 he married Corinne and has two children, Harry and Charlotte. He is CEO and owner of Came & Company, insurance brokers since 1995, employing ten people.

In 2010 he became Hampshire Hogs' leading run scoring batsman of all time, beating the previous best, Michael Moldon, who made 10,156 runs. Now Peter is already well ahead and he has many more years playing for the club.

Rupert Fiennes-Cox

Rupert Cox was a stocky left-hander who was on Hampshire's books between 1986 and 1994. While he performed with a compelling smile on his face, he lacked the range of strokes to elevate him to the top echelons of county cricket. Proud of his inspiring schooling at Cheam School and Bradfield College, he captained England Schools South X1 against Michael Atherton's northern rivals, before captaining Hampshire under-19s. He initially struggled to make his mark in Hampshire's second X1, until in 1990 an avalanche of runs, including five centuries, enabled him to make his first-class debut at Arundel. At Worcester, a month later, as a 22-year-old, he struck his only first-class century in just 133 balls, as, in partnership with Tony Middleton, he helped Hampshire recover from an awkward position. But David Gower and Robin Smith returned from a Test match and he was dropped for the next fixture. He scored more runs in the second XI than anyone previously in a season, beating Robin Smith's record.

Sadly, it marked the high point of his career. The desire to succeed and his own weight of expectation hung too heavily upon him. So when, at 26, he played consecutive first-class matches for the first time he failed to deliver. He speaks fondly of his cricket memories and the camaraderie he so enjoyed. He accepts that while a good team man, he did not have the requisite selfishness to be a better batsman. Strangely, he remembers an unbeaten 107 in a second X1 one-day semi-final against Leicestershire, in a low-scoring and losing cause, as his best and most imperious innings. Out of professional cricket at 27, he was fortunate to be able to relax and enjoy an abundance of social cricket with Hampshire Hogs, Free Foresters, MCC and Bradfield Waifs. County cricket's loss is the amateurs' gain, for now he coaches and quietly passes on his wisdom on each of the disciplines. Acknowledged as a brilliant fielder and very useful medium change bowler, in his element in the dressing room, he always provides an abundance of good humour for all to enjoy. He wrote freelance for The Times between 1995 and 2001 before he became managing director of two companies in Newbury, Berkshire, selling coffee machines and water coolers for Circon. He is married to Daniela, lives in Hampshire and has two children, Oliver and Isabella. Rupert is a born leader, a natural coach and a kind and generous friend.

Jonathan Grant

Jonathan Grant is an all rounder in every sense of the word. He represented his prep school in every team except chess, winning the Victor Ludorum when 12 and when 13 was twice Sussex u-13 breaststroke swimming champion. On reaching Marlborough College, he played cricket for the first XI and the squash V, and then gained a degree in Business Studies and Computers.

He became an investment banker (securities trader) for seven years, from whence he bought a business franchise, selling it after five years. He has not neglected his sporting interest. When aged 18, he joined Hampshire Hogs and was fixtures' secretary for 13 years. Despite never having time to practice, he has featured in the club's opening partnership record on three occasions, the latest when, with Tom Cledwyn, he put on 289 in 2005.

Jonathan is married to Kate and has three lovely daughters – Jemima, Polly and Aliza. He is fun loving, kind and generous of nature with a great sense of humour, but above all he is a loyal and true friend.

This section is almost impossible to write as there have been many Hampshire Hogs' friends who at different times have been special to me and my wife. To name them all would be incongruous and there would always be someone who one missed, that might be hurtful, in consequence I ask that those who know they are special to us take this as a blanket 'THANK YOU' and hope you understand.

Two people who deserve to be named are Jenny and Rob

White, together and separately they have been wonderful to this club, giving away hours of time and dedication to the cause and both have been an inspiration and shown immeasurable kindness to both myself and my wife.

Apart from The Hogs, The Bat & Ball CC has been very important to me, there have been many people who have shared its success and given me support and kindness who I also thank – particular amongst them have been Barrie and Joan Hunter, Dick and Lesley Orders, Richard and Liz Gale, Keith and Liz Ellis, Iain Tait and Max Craft, Sandra and Jason Eastlake and Roger Vernier.

APPENDIX 2

In Praise of the Wicket-Keeper

He is the fulcrum of every team when in the field. His prowess will increase the ability of each bowler, or fielder, support the captain and his performance can turn the game.

He must keep his concentration for every ball. He is the vital back up for every slow bowler. Within my cricketing life I would like to pay tribute to the following 'keepers, in no particular order:

Hampshire Hogs
John Hawkings-Byass
Charles Gabb
Christopher Laine
Rob Kitson
Nick Smith
Christopher Anderson
Dominic Allom
Kevin Foyle
Stephen Lapage
Nick Rowsell
Tony Snook
Tim Beecroft
Toby Harris
Robert Harris
Paul Bailey
Mark Mackenzie-Crooks
Henry Marks
Archie Fellowes

Hardye's School
Adrian Downton
Colin Roper
Broadhalfpenny Brigands
Richard Fortin
The Forty Club
Ted Brown
John Harris
Mike Vimpany
Hambledon
Chris de Mellow
Peter Tompkins
12th Men
Andy Brown
Auckland Cricket Society
Noel Plumer
The Bat and Ball
Alan Fisher
Barry Smith

APPENDIX 3

The Bazalgette Family

By Christopher Bazalgette

My great grandfather was Sir Joseph William Bazalgette, world famous for being the civil engineer who removed typhoid and cholera from the River Thames in 1858. He achieved this mammoth task by creating a system of inter- connecting sewage tunnels for central London, so taking the sewage off the streets. Owing to the lie of the land, it was also necessary to build pumping stations. Thus sewage stopped seeping directly into the Thames and was channelled to enter the river much nearer the estuary.

When he created the drawings and later the budget for this engineering feat, he had the foresight to magnify it by six times. Now, 150 years later, many of his sewers are still coping with the demands of the present day.

He was the chief of the Metropolitan Board and his works included the Albert, Chelsea and Victoria Embankments; his bust can be seen on the latter. He designed the Maidstone, Albert, Putney, Hammersmith, Battersea and Tower bridges and the Woolwich Free Ferry. He was also responsible for Northumberland Avenue, Shaftesbury Avenue, Garrick Street and Charing Cross Road. He was made president of the Institute of Civil Engineers in 1883.

One of his great grandsons was Squadron Leader Ian Willoughby Bazalgette DFC VC, who gained his posthumous VC in France in 1944.

Another great great grandson is Peter 'Baz' Bazalgette, who was president of the Cambridge Union and created hits for British TV from his own production company, BAZAL, such as Ready, Steady, Cook,. Changing Rooms and Work Force.

He popularised the format around the world for Big Brother and became Chairman of Endemol (UK) in 2005, Later, he was creative director of Endemol Group worldwide, responsible for Big Brother and Deal or No Deal, which were hits around the world.

He was a former Board member of Channel 4 and a non-executive director of YouGov, as well as a board member of English National Opera and deputy chairman of the UK National Film and Television School. He became a British media expert and was the leading creative figure in the Global TV company, Endemol.

He co-wrote four books including The Food Revolution – You don't have to diet, and Billion Dollar Game.

Other distinguished family members are Adam Bazalgette, who was formerly Director of David Leadbetter's Golf Academy for thirteen years, Mark Bazalgette, who is a colorectal surgeon in Seattle. Simon Bazalgette who is group Chief Executive of the Jockey Club. Christopher John Bazalgette a Technical Consultant in website optimisation, author and Poet.

APPENDIX 4

The Forty Club

In 1977 Arthur Holt invited me to join The Forty Club (the largest amateur cricket club in the world with over 3900 members), Arthur was on the Executive Committee and South District Chairman, The Forty Club was founded in 1936 by Henry Grierson (Cambridge University and Bedfordshire). Its aim was, and remains, to take cricket to the schools by offering them fixtures against experienced cricketers who would encourage schoolboys to play the game to the highest standards of behaviour and performance and in the best spirit of the game. England was split into a number of districts plus one for Scotland and Wales. I played in a number of matches across the South of England and in 1993 I became District Chairman for the South, making me responsible for the playing of 19 matches, arranging the Managers, who would also recruit for the club. The district covered four counties plus the Isle of Wight and the Channel Islands. This position I held for 9 years. In 1992 I was co-opted onto the Executive Committee, almost immediately I was asked to chair the marketing committee, this I did for three years, I was lucky to have Carl Openshaw (who went on to become Chairman and then President of Kent CCC) and Ron Hart (a former director of Whitbread) and a consummate Public Relations and press expert Sam Luckin to support and guide me in committee. Then in 2001 I was elected to Chair the Cricket Committee, a much-coveted appointment, this post I held till 2005. I was proud to write the first Newsletter and I created the Inter-District Knockout Competition, I also led the South District to win the event in its second year, beating the West District.

I decided in 2005 to retire from the Executive and as Cricket Chairman, as I felt the job required a more youthful approach. In 2006 the Club honoured me by making me an Honorary Fellow.

John Williams, a friend of mine was Chairman of the West District and on the Executive, he was most supportive in my early days and when I started my Executive roles. Many people helped me, David Hamilton and Peter Bown were very special Hon. Secretaries whose council was often sought and neither of them ever failed to provide the perfect answer,

Jack Hyde-Blake encouraged me and gave me confidence to take responsibility. I know the club is in good hands, as two friends I proposed for the club are now Hon. Chairman and Hon. Secretary – Barrie Hunter and Barry Aitken respectively. However one person has held her position as Membership secretary for over twenty six years, her dedication, friendship and kindness has been far beyond the call of duty, she has always been there for me, for the club and all the officers, Well Done Paddy Gaywood. I hope the MCC give her the full membership she deserves, actually for her dedicated service to cricket for around forty years she should be recognised in the Honours List.

APPENDIX 5

Lord Bramall

Field Marshall Edwin Noel Westby Bramall, Baron Bramall was educated at Eton College and commissioned in 1943, in the King's Royal Rifle Corps. He fought in the 2nd World War between 1944 and 1945, in north west Europe. He was decorated with the Military Cross in 1945. He was invested as an Officer, Order of the British Empire in 1965. He was Commanding Officer of the 2nd Green Jackets, King's Royal Rifle Corps between 1965 and 1966 in Malaysia. He was Commanding Officer of the 5th Airportable Brigade in 1967 and 1969 and he was Commanding Officer of the 1st Division, British Army of the Rhine between 1971 and 1973 and was promoted to Lieutenant-General in 1973. He then was Commander of the British Forces between 1973 and 1976 in Hong Kong.

Also from 1973 to 1984 he was Colonel Commandant of the 3rd Battalion, Royal Green Jackets.

He was then invested as a Knight Commander, Order of the Bath, (KCB) in 1974. He gained the rank of General in 1976, and became Colonel of the 2nd Gurkhas in 1977. Next was another title this was as a Knight Grand Cross, Order of the Bath in 1979 (GCB), In 1982 he rose to Field Marshall. In 1986 he was invested as a Knight, Most Venerable Order of the Hospital of St John of Jerusalem (K.St.J.) and was also JP for London in the same year. Further he was made Lord-Lieutenant of Greater London for the next twelve years, the following year–1987 He was created as a Life Peer – Baron Bramall of Bushfield in the County of Hampshire. Then in 1990 he was invested as a Knight, Order of the Garter (KG). He was co-author of the book *The Chiefs* in 1993.

Christopher Bazalgette's Career
amateur cricket

Clubs played for:
- M.C.C.
- Hon.Fellow The Forty Club
- Life member Hampshire Hogs
- Berkshire Gentlemen
- Life member Devon Dumplings
- Hon. Life member Hambledon CC.
- Jt. Founder & Hon. Life President The Bat & Ball CC
- The Grannies CC
- The Duke of Richmond's XI (300th Anniversary)
- Bracknell CC
- Headley CC
- Farnham CC
- Broadhalfpenny Brigands CC
- Upwey & Broadway CC
- Havant Wednesday
- Hampshire over 50s
- Hon. Life member Hinton Admiral CC
- Elvino's
- Old Honitonians – Life member
- Hardye's School
- *The Cricketer* International in the UK and Corfu
- The Household Cavalry
- Hampshire Maniacs
- Overseas Clubs membership:
- The Crusaders – Hon. Life member (Australia)
- The Willows – Hon. Overseas member (NZ)

Also played for:

- Auckland Cricket Society (NZ)
- Auckland Police (NZ)
- The Fingletoads (NZ)

- Toured South Africa and Australia with the Hogs.
- Toured The Channel Isles with Hampshire CCC.

BIBLIOGRAPHY

The Croucher - The Biography of Gilbert Jessop, Gerald Broadribb, London Magazines 1974

Head On - Ian Botham's Autobiography, Ebury Press (Ebury Publishers, 2007

Fit for a Queen, Richard Pitman, Pride of Place (UK) Ltd., 1995

Royal Champion, Bill Curling, Michael Joseph (London), 1980

The Hennessey Gold Cup, Stewart Peters, Tempus Publishing, 2006

Lords of Cricket, Jocelyn Galsworthy & Judy Vigors, The Sportsman's Press, 2005

Beyond the Airing Cupboard, John Barclay's Autobiography, Fairfield Books, 2008

INDEX

Please Note: As there are many references to The Marylebone Cricket Club, Hampshire Hogs CC and Hampshire CCC, we decided not to index them.